In Search of Timothy

Discovering and Developing Greatness in
Church Staff and Volunteers

Tony Cooke

...But whoever desires to become great among you, let him be your servant. And whoever desires to be first among you, let him be your slave—just as the Son of Man did not come to be served, but to serve, and to give His life a ransom for many.

Matthew 20:26–28

These things I write to you, though I hope to come to you shortly; but if I am delayed, I write so that you may know how you ought to conduct yourself in the house of God, which is the church of the living God, the pillar and ground of the truth.

1 Timothy 3:14–15

Second Printing 2005

ISBN 0-89276-973-4

In the U.S. write:
Kenneth Hagin Ministries
P.O. Box 50126
Tulsa, OK 74150-0126
1-888-28-FAITH
www.rhema.org

In Canada write:
Kenneth Hagin Ministries
P.O. Box 335, Station D
Etobicoke (Toronto), Ontario
Canada, M9A 4X3

C O N T E N T S

I write this book with great appreciation for having worked on two excellent church staffs over a twenty-year period. I will always be grateful to Dr. Dan Beller and Pastor Kenneth Hagin Jr. for the opportunity to have served them in their respective ministries; the training I received from them was invaluable. Serving on these church staffs taught me the value of partnership, provided insights on working with people possessing different and complementary gifts, and enabled me to see the power of teamwork in operation.

While I learned many valuable lessons from my time on staff with these two outstanding pastors, much of the information included in this book was gleaned during my time as director of RHEMA Ministerial Association International. My time as RMAI director afforded me hundreds upon hundreds of conversations with various pastors concerning their experiences with staff members and supportive ministers. I also had countless conversations with various staff members concerning their experiences in their respective ministries.

I'm also thankful for the countless interactions I've experienced with other leaders throughout my years of traveling and ministering in many states and various countries. All of these interactions throughout my time in ministry have given me numerous windows into church staff issues, giving me the opportunity to observe both positive and negative aspects of ministry relationships.

I know that staff and supportive ministry relationships are not always positive. A seasoned authority in church growth and leadership issues shared the following sobering observation:

> My thirty-five years of involvement with hundreds of church multiple staffs is most depressing. It is rare to find one out of four multiple staffs working in love and harmony. Many team members merely tolerate each other. They resemble married couples living together like singles who have no commitment, common goals, or sense of sharing. They simply share the same house.

If there is any place in the Christian world where people ought to be a genuine team, it is in the leadership of the church. The pastoral staff should be a model of all that Christ intended the Church to be. To please the Father is to work in unity. Church leadership should demonstrate the genuine working out of diversity of gifts. The pastoral staff should show how acceptance, forgiveness, sharing, supporting, encouraging, and the accomplishment of common goals is practiced. The staff must be a microcosm of the body of Christ, a church in miniature. If the pastoral staff can't demonstrate to God's people the beauty and harmony of the body of Christ, its members can't expect the church family to function together adequately.[1]

This book can be read by an individual with great benefit, but I believe the greatest benefit of *In Search of Timothy* will be found in group study and discussion. I envision church staffs and leadership teams reading this book as a "staff devotional" and then using the Questions for Reflection and Discussion at the end of each chapter for group discussion. I believe that doing so will help produce the results described in Hebrews 10:24 and 25: "And let us consider and give attentive, continuous care to watching over one another, studying how we may stir up (stimulate and incite) to love and helpful deeds and noble activities, Not forsaking or neglecting to assemble together [as believers], as is the habit of some people, but admonishing (warning, urging, and encouraging) one another, and all the more faithfully as you see the day approaching" (*Amplified*).

I recognize that contributions in the Body of Christ come from both men and women. Any references in this book to a pastor, leader, or worker as "him" or "he" is stated generically and is not meant to exclude the vital work of women in the Church—both in leadership and supportive roles. I am simply avoiding the usage of phrases such as "him or her" and "he or she," which can become awkward when used repeatedly.

Finally, in reading this book, please keep in mind that I am presenting many *ideals*. We are all at different levels of growth, maturity, development, and even commitment. The content of this book is not meant to be an ironclad, rigid standard against which people are judged and condemned for not measuring up.

I pray that this book will be read and applied with grace, understanding that we are all growing and that we are all a work in progress. If God had to wait until we were absolutely perfect before He could use us, none of us could serve Him. At the same time, I trust that those reading this book will aspire to be the best they can be for the Kingdom of God and will seek to grow into all that God has for them. Our development takes time, but with God's help, we will always be increasing in our value and contribution to His Kingdom.

Tony Cooke

---

[1] Taken from *Church Staff Handbook*, 2nd ed., © 1997 by Harold J. Westing. Published by Kregel Publications, Grand Rapids, MI. Used by permission of the publisher. All rights reserved.

W hy the title—*In Search of Timothy*? Leaders are *searching* (many times with a sense of desperation) for workers who will be loyal and faithful and provide quality service. This book details the qualities every leader longs to find within his staff and other key leaders. It is my prayer that those reading these pages will *search* within themselves to see how they can increase the quality of service they are providing to their pastors, leaders, and to the Body of Christ.

Why search for *Timothy*? Timothy stands out as a sterling example of how supportive ministers can serve and assist leaders in the Body of Christ. The way Timothy served and assisted Paul was never meant to be enshrined as an isolated or unique case. Rather, Timothy is a great pattern for every Christian to follow and emulate as supportive ministers and team players. Timothy is one of a great company in Scripture who served God by assisting others, and he remains as an example for those who are serving leaders today.

Since the term *supportive minister* is used extensively throughout this book, let's define it here at the very beginning. Something that is *supportive* provides stability and lends strength; it undergirds and assists. A *minister* is one who serves God and others. Therefore, the term *supportive minister* describes any person who assists another, provides stability, lends strength, undergirds, and offers support through serving.

The principles I am addressing are generally applicable whether a person is paid by the church or whether he volunteers. Obviously, those who are employed on a full-time basis will typically have a broader, more intense job description, but God wants everyone serving Him to exhibit excellence and a servant's heart regardless of whether he is financially compensated or not.

Why is staff unity such a priority to God? He knows that unity releases awesome potential.

After the flood, Noah's descendants undertook an ambitious building project, and God made this observation: "Behold, they are one people and they have all one language; and this is only the beginning of what they will do, and now nothing they have imagined they can do will be impossible for them" (Gen. 11:6 *Amplified*). God recognized the limitless possibility unity affords and put a stop to the unified efforts to build the Tower of Babel because the people had a carnal agenda.

Unity is a good thing when aimed in the right direction; it is a powerful, positive force when people unite for the right cause. Churches today will be able to achieve the unimaginable—what others would consider impossible—when leadership teams are united in their commitment to serve the Lord Jesus Christ!

Throughout the Bible we see God consistently working through teams of two or more people to accomplish His will and His purpose.

Moses functioned in partnership with Joshua, Aaron, Hur, and the elders.

Jonathan and other "mighty men" were a part of what God did through David.

Elisha worked with Elijha.

Jesus had a team of twelve disciples.

Paul had working relationships with many people: Timothy, Barnabas, Luke, Silas, Titus, Mark, and others.

We learn through Scripture that these leaders were never meant to be isolated as they fulfilled God's will; they were designed to function in teams and in partnership with others. It is my heartfelt prayer that this book will help raise up a new generation of supportive ministers who have the same kind of heart and attitude as Timothy, and will also enhance the performance and raise the quality of service being given by those already functioning in supportive ministry positions.

The Bible places great value on those who serve in supportive roles, and I write with great respect and appreciation for all those who serve behind the scenes. They are often the unsung heroes in the church. Pastors realize that without the partnership and involvement of supportive ministers, the effectiveness of church ministry would dramatically decline. I believe we'll be surprised in heaven at the honor and rewards God gives to those who may have never preached a sermon, but who served faithfully and diligently in a wide variety of supportive ministry positions.

May we all strive to become more like Timothy as we serve our respective leaders and at the same time continue to become more like Jesus as we minister God's love to those around us.

PART I

Biblical Principles of Supportive Ministry

In this first part of *In Search of Timothy*, we will study various biblical principles of supportive ministry. These principles have spiritual and practical application and will begin to convey the magnitude of importance which God places upon supportive ministers and their ministry. Yes, it is indeed a ministry, and supportive ministers have no need to feel second-rate.

It's been said, "The person who says he is leading but has no followers is only taking a walk." Every good leader requires good followers. Putting these principles into practice will empower and equip you to be the good follower every leader wants and to become the "Timothy" your pastor is searching for.

The Challenges of Leadership

A spiritual leader I know had a large congregation. Everything seemed fine until one of his top staff members—one of his key assistants—decided he could do things better. The assistant took more than 30 percent of the congregation and started his own work. Needless to say, it was a painful split.

(When this type of thing occurs, questions are asked. The armchair quarterbacks begin their second-guessing: "If only the leader had been more connected with his staff, this wouldn't have happened." Or, "If only the leader had developed a better relationship with his congregation, such a large percentage wouldn't have been susceptible to being pulled away.")

After the split, the leader maintained his work with the part of the congregation that remained, and it was still a good-sized group. But the leader also decided to go ahead and pioneer a new work—another congregation in a different location. Like most new works, this one was small, very small in fact, but the leader saw great potential in this fledgling group. This time, a split did not occur. It was *worse*. This time, the leader lost his *entire* congregation.

The leader later did some things that enabled him to recapture some of that lost congregation and to rebuild it even larger, but the whole process was not without challenges and setbacks. A lot of blood, sweat, and tears went into the rebuilding process.

This first leader had a close relative who also went into the ministry. He had a true shepherd's heart and was an excellent teacher. The Spirit's Presence was with him in a remarkable way, and he got great results. However, he also faced challenges in his leadership. He had a lot of turnover—people came and went on a regular basis. He had retention problems, and on one occasion there was a mass exodus from his congregation.

This leader also had challenges with his staff. His top staff members didn't always get along well. They were competitive and had periodic arguments among themselves. It was later discovered that he had a staff member who was actually involved in embezzling ministry funds. He had another staff member who was known for being impulsive in both word and deed. This individual "lost it" one time under pressure and actually assaulted another person.

Because you have enough interest in supportive ministry to pick up this book, there are some questions I'd like you to consider:

- Would you want to work on the staff of one of the afore-mentioned leaders?
- Would you want to work for a leader who loses more than 30 percent of his congregation, then starts a new work and has the whole thing go under (at least temporarily)?
- Would you want to work for a leader whose staff doesn't always get along well and where there's a high turnover rate among the congregation?

Who Are These Leaders?

The first leader I described is God the Father. The second leader is Jesus. I shared their history in a slightly veiled and disguised way on purpose. We would all agree that God the Father and Jesus are wonderful—perfect in every way. Yet they both encountered problems in their leadership.

God's archangel Lucifer rebelled against Him and took one-third of the angels. Later, Adam and Eve (God's second "congregation") turned against God, and as the representative

> GOD THE FATHER AND JESUS ARE WONDERFUL—PERFECT IN EVERY WAY. YET THEY BOTH ENCOUNTERED PROBLEMS IN THEIR LEADERSHIP.

heads of the human race broke relationship and fellowship with Him. Of course, to say that Jesus' disciples were rough around the edges is to put it mildly.

Were the problems we described problems of *leadership*, or problems of *follower-ship*? Was it that God the Father and Jesus failed to exercise good leadership, or that others failed to exercise good follower-ship? Again, we know that God and Jesus are both perfect and infallible. Therefore, their leadership skills leave nothing to be desired. *But good leadership can't achieve optimum results without good follower-ship.*

Good Leaders Need Good Followers

No doubt, leadership is a huge issue. We've been privileged to have some excellent teaching on leadership in the Body of Christ over the past several years, and thank God for it. Leaders must lead, and we are

> GOOD LEADERSHIP CAN'T ACHIEVE OPTIMUM RESULTS WITHOUT GOOD FOLLOWER-SHIP.

grateful for all the vital truths that help leaders develop their skills to lead more effectively. But followers also have a part to play. They must seek to excel in following and in faithfully carrying out their own duties and responsibilities.

Paul's statement in Romans 1:11 and 12 illustrates this point.

ROMANS 1:11–12
11 **For I long to see you, that I may impart to you some spiritual gift, so that you may be established—**
12 **that is, that I may be encouraged together with you by the mutual faith both of you and me.**

Notice how Paul began his letter to the Church at Rome. As a leader, he automatically thought of what he could do to serve and to help the believers, and what he wrote in verse 11 essentially reflects this "one-way street" mentality. He says, in effect, "I'm going to come and impart something to you, and it's going to help you."

But then Paul realizes that his ministry isn't a one-way street. In effect, Paul says in verse 12, "It's not just me giving to you, but we need to work together in this matter. There's a mutual give-and-take here. I've got to do my part, but you've got to do your part also, and when we mutually do our jobs, then we're all going to be blessed and encouraged."

It's not just leadership that's going to get the job done. Follower-ship is a big part of the equation as well. There's no doubt that good leadership helps to inspire and motivate good follower-ship. But good follower-ship encourages good leadership as well. When both parties function well, it raises all of us higher.

QUESTIONS FOR REFLECTION AND DISCUSSION

1. What was your reaction when you realized that the two leaders described early in the chapter were God the Father and Jesus?
2. What are your thoughts about the leadership/follower-ship challenges God and Jesus faced?
3. What do you think about the statement, "Good leadership can't achieve optimum results without good follower-ship"?
4. What are your reflections about Romans 1:11–12? ("For I long to see you, that I may impart to you some spiritual gift, so that you may be established—that is, that I may be encouraged together with you by the mutual faith both of you and me.")
5. What did you learn from this chapter and how can you apply it?
6. What areas do you need to pray about or improve in?

The Voices of
Lonely Leaders

There is an old saying, "It's lonely at the top." Whoever coined that phrase could have been reflecting on the lives and ministries of the great leaders of the Bible. In both the Old and New Testaments, we see leaders who endured a great lack of support and felt very alone in carrying out the assignment God had given them, at least until they benefited from the partnership of those who were assigned to help them. Many of today's leaders face the same challenges. They are searching for divinely assigned people to partner with them to help them carry out the vision they have received.

Paul: A Lonely Apostle?

In Paul's final epistle, we receive amazing insight into the life of the great apostle. We often think of Paul in terms of the outstanding revelation he received from God and recorded in his letters, of the many churches he planted, and of the staggering persecutions he endured. What we often fail to see is the sense of alone-ness and the lack of support he experienced at times while straining toward the finish line of his ministry.
Consider Paul's comments from Second Timothy:
• *"This you know, that all those in Asia have turned away from me, among whom are Phygellus and Hermogenes"* (2 Tim. 1:15).

• *"For Demas has forsaken me, having loved this present world, and has departed for Thessalonica..."* (2 Tim. 4:10).
• *"At my first defense no one stood with me, but all forsook me. May it not be charged against them"* (2 Tim. 4:16).

GOD NEVER INTENDED FOR US TO BE ALONE OR TO TRY TO DO EVERYTHING BY OURSELVES. WE NEED OTHER PEOPLE.

When Paul's supporters forsook him during his difficult days, he called out for an old friend, his protégé and son in the faith. He was searching for Timothy. From the restrictions and limitations of his Roman cell where he was held prisoner, Paul made the following requests:

• *"Be diligent to come to me quickly"* (2 Tim. 4:9).
• *"Bring the cloak that I left with Carpus at Troas when you come—and the books, especially the parchments"* (2 Tim. 4:13).
• *"Do your utmost to come before winter..."* (2 Tim. 4:21).

These are not mere directives routinely spoken; they are the heartfelt pleas of a man who desperately needed Timothy. Consider the very vivid and graphic insights provided in Charles Swindoll's imaginative amplification of Paul's words from prison:

> I need my cloak. I must have left it at the abode of Carpus in Troas. You'll have no trouble spotting it, Timothy. It's an old thing, but it's been on my back through many a bitter winter. It's been wet with the brine of the Great Sea, white with the snows of the rugged peaks of Pamphylia, gritty and brown from the dust of the Egnatian Way, and crimson with my own blood from that awful stoning at Lystra. The cloak is stained and torn, Timothy, but winter's coming and I need the warmth it will bring.
>
> I also need the books. You remember them. The ones I read under candlelight as we rode out the rough waters of the Agean and endured the rigors of Macedonia together...those scrolls that fed my mind with fresh

bursts of hope and stimulating ideas. Bring along those books, my friend. I especially need the parchments!

> THERE WAS A REASON PAUL CALLED OUT FOR TIMOTHY WHEN HE NEEDED SOMEONE THE MOST.

Those are my most treasured possessions, Timothy. How I need the comfort of King David's psalms, the fortitude from the prophets' pens, the insights and perceptions from Solomon's proverbs. Yes, the parchments. Surely they will help keep my heart warm and my hopes high in this desolate place.

But Timothy, I need you. How desperately I need you! Make every effort to come...come before winter. Come before November's winds strip the leaves from the trees and send them whirling across the fields and swirling through the busy streets above me. Come, before the snow begins to fall and covers flat carts and frozen ponds with its icy blanket. Come, my friend... the time of my departure has arrived. Soon the blade will drop and time for me will be no more. I cannot bear the thought of midwinter without the warmth of your companionship...those eyes of understanding, those words only you can bring to get me through this barren and bitter season. Make every effort to come before winter.[1]

There was a reason Paul called out for *Timothy* when he needed someone the most. Paul trusted and valued Timothy— as a friend and as a fellow minister. Why Timothy? Throughout the rest of this book, we will discover and study the characteristics that made Timothy so special to Paul and to the Body of Christ.

No One Else Like Timothy

Paul sensed a lack of support and assistance at other times in his ministry, not just during his final days on earth. Many years before Paul penned Second Timothy, Paul revealed this lack of support in a letter he wrote to the Philippians during his first Roman imprisonment.

Paul dearly loved the believers at Philippi; they had never given him the frustrations and heartaches he had experienced with the Christians in Galatia and Corinth. Though separated from the Philippians by hundreds of miles, Paul's heart was nevertheless with them. He wanted to visit them personally but was unable to do so because he was in prison. Instead, Paul wrote to them and said the following:

PHILIPPIANS 2:19–21

19 But I trust in the Lord Jesus to send Timothy to you shortly, that I also may be encouraged when I know your state.

20 FOR I HAVE NO ONE LIKE-MINDED, who will sincerely care for your state.

21 For all seek their own, not the things which are of Christ Jesus

The *New Living Translation* renders verse 20 this way, "I have no one else like Timothy." And the *Amplified* says, "For I have no one like him [no one of so kindred a spirit]."

When you hear Paul's deep longings for the Christians in Philippi, you are immediately aware of the restrictions and limitations he faced. He wanted to be with them. He wanted to be reassured that they were doing well and that they were abiding in the faith. He wanted to know that they were being cared for and ministered to properly.

However, due to his imprisonment, Paul needed someone who could serve as a bridge between him and the Philippians. He needed a representative—someone who could go as an extension and expression of himself, someone to go in his stead and be a true reflection of his heart toward the Philippians. It couldn't be just anyone; a hireling would not meet the need. It had to be someone who would genuinely care for these precious believers and seek their best interests in the same way Paul would have. Paul only had one person who could do this—and it was *Timothy*.

Thank God that Paul had Timothy, but I wonder why Paul only had one person he could trust to that degree. Why did the most influential minister in the history of Christianity only have one person available to assist him in this difficult situation? Shouldn't there have been dozens of young ministers, eager to serve and to sacrifice alongside the great apostle?

Remember, it's lonely at the top. Or, from the standpoint of servanthood, we should say, "It's lonely at the bottom." When you study the Bible you find that Paul was not the first believer to sense isolation and alone-ness in endeavoring to carry out the will of God.

Moses: A Do-It-Yourself Kind of Guy

In Exodus chapter 18, Moses was trying to conduct an enormous amount of ministry by himself. As admirable as Moses' intentions were (to help people), his tendency of trying to do everything himself was actually an invitation for frustration and exhaustion. Moses worked from early morning until late at night, trying to handle every person's problems and disputes on his own.

Fortunately for himself and for us, Moses had a wise and insightful father-in-law. Moses' father-in-law, Jethro, saw what was happening and made the following observation:

EXODUS 18:17–18

17 So Moses' father-in-law said to him, "The thing that you do is not good.

18 Both you and these people who are with you will surely wear yourselves out. FOR THIS THING IS TOO MUCH FOR YOU; YOU ARE NOT ABLE TO PERFORM IT BY YOURSELF.

As much as we may want to do things on our own, the Bible teaches that "doing it all" isn't good for us. According to verse 18, always being a "do-it-all-yourself" kind of person will surely wear you out and also wear out the people who are with you.

On another occasion, Moses became extremely distressed after a time of intense complaining by the people. You can sense his deep frustration when he spoke to the Lord in Numbers chapter 11.

NUMBERS 11:11–12,14–15

11 So Moses said to the Lord, "Why have You afflicted Your servant? And why have I not found favor in Your sight, that You have laid the burden of all these people on me?

12 Did I conceive all these people? Did I beget them, that You should say to me, 'Carry them in your bosom, as a guardian carries a nursing child,' to the land which You swore to their fathers?

14 I AM NOT ABLE TO BEAR ALL THESE PEOPLE ALONE, BECAUSE THE BURDEN IS TOO HEAVY FOR ME.

15 IF YOU TREAT ME LIKE THIS, PLEASE KILL ME HERE AND NOW—if I have found favor in Your sight—and do not let me see my wretchedness!"

This is some heavy-duty frustration! Moses felt so isolated in his ministry that he expressed a desire to die to avoid having to continually face the burden of carrying the people alone.

Elijah: Alone and Discouraged

Elijah was another man whom God used mightily, but Elijah came to a place where he was painfully isolated in his work for the Lord. Following the miraculous victory over the prophets of Baal, Elijah received a death threat from Queen Jezebel. Discouragement and despair overwhelmed him, and, like Moses, Elijah expressed a desire to die.

1 KINGS 19:4,10

4 **...And HE PRAYED THAT HE MIGHT DIE, and said, "It is enough! Now, Lord, TAKE MY LIFE, for I am no better than my fathers!"**

10 **So he said, "I have been very zealous for the Lord God of hosts; for the children of Israel have forsaken Your covenant, torn down Your altars, and killed Your prophets with the sword. I ALONE AM LEFT; and they seek to take my life."**

In his distress, Elijah expressed his feelings of being alone in his work for the Lord. This "alone-ness" led to intense discouragement—so intense in fact that in that moment Elijah thought he would be better off dead.

God never intended for us to be alone or to try to do everything by ourselves. *We need other people.* Even *Jesus* needed other people.

Jesus: Deserted by His Disciples

When Jesus went to the Garden of Gethsemane and suffered the soul-anguish that preceded His crucifixion, He asked His main group of disciples to stay in one place and took Peter, James, and John with Him a little farther into the garden. Throughout His agonizing time in prayer, Jesus kept going back to these three disciples but repeatedly found them sleeping. He said to them, *"What! Could you not watch with Me one hour?"* (Matt. 26:40), or, as the *Message* version renders it, "Can't you stick it out with me a single hour?"

Jesus knew that Peter, James, and John couldn't change the situation He was destined to face. But it seems Jesus was looking for comfort, consolation, and companionship from His closest associates during His hour of greatest need. And the three disciples didn't deliver.

Each of these spiritual leaders—Paul, Moses, Elijah, and Jesus—experienced a sense of alone-ness as they endeavored to carry out their God-given assignments. There were different reasons why each leader felt this way. In Paul's case we read that people were too self-centered and self-focused to serve sacrificially. Moses and Elijah had a tendency to do everything themselves. Jesus was left alone because Peter, James, and John failed to perceive the magnitude of what was happening in their midst (not only in the Garden of Gethsemane, but also on the Mount of Transfiguration—it appears they slept through at least some of that experience as well according to Luke 9:32).

Each of these cases I've mentioned is a fairly dramatic example, and it's easy for us to say what we would have done if we had been in the exact situation. "If I had been alive back then, I would have helped Moses and Elijah." "I would have stayed awake and offered support for Jesus in the Garden." "I would have been right there with Timothy helping Paul."

The reality, though, is that we *can't* support Paul, Moses, Elijah, or Jesus in their earthly ministries. They've finished their work here and have passed on to their rewards. But there *are* a multitude of spiritual leaders ministering today who *do* need support. There are pastors in every community in our country (and around the world) who need others to support and assist them in their work for God. Countless pastors today—at this very hour—are in search of Timothy!

QUESTIONS FOR REFLECTION AND DISCUSSION

1. What does the saying, "It's lonely at the top" mean?
2. What are some biblical examples of that saying?
3. What are some of the different reasons why various biblical leaders faced a sense of alone-ness in their respective ministries?
4. Does your pastor feel surrounded and supported by a great team of staff, leaders, and workers who are actively sharing and helping in carrying out the vision God has put in his heart?
5. Why might your pastor sense some of the alone-ness that many of the great leaders of the Bible sensed?

6. What did you learn from this chapter and how can you apply it?
7. What areas do you need to pray about or improve in?

---

[1] Charles R. Swindoll, *Come Before Winter and Share My Hope* (Wheaton, IL: Living Books / Tyndale, 1985), 12–13. Used by permission of the publisher.

Learning to Be Like Timothy

When Lisa and I first went to Bible school I had certain ideas and aspirations about how God would use us in future ministry. But instead of placing us in a high-visibility position (such as pulpit ministry), the Lord wisely placed us where we could grow in character and learn the value and importance of serving. Serving as a janitor in a local church brought several issues to the surface in my life: I had immaturities and pride that needed to be addressed and dealt with, and I needed to cultivate a servant's heart. I needed to become more like Timothy.

There were times when my attitude was not what it should have been, and the Lord graciously spoke three vital words of instruction and correction to my heart. Those three corrections became my core values and shaped my view of supportive ministry from that time forward.

Correction #1:
Be Faithful in the 'Little'

The first time the Lord corrected me, He said, "I want you to treat this job as though it were your ultimate calling and as though it were the most important thing you could ever do for Me."

Sometimes what we consider "little," or insignificant, is something upon which God places great value. In Luke 16:10, Jesus taught the importance of exercising faithfulness in seemingly small things.

LUKE 16:10–12 *(NIV)*

10 Whoever can be trusted with very little can also be trusted with much, and whoever is dishonest with very little will also be dishonest with much.

11 So if you have not been trustworthy in handling worldly wealth, who will trust you with true riches?

12 And if you have not been trustworthy with someone else's property, who will give you property of your own?

> SOMETIMES PEOPLE SEE WHAT THEY ARE CURRENTLY DOING AS A MERE STEPPING-STONE TO SOMETHING ELSE—TO THE GREENER GRASS ON THE OTHER SIDE OF THE FENCE.

God may be more interested in *our faithfulness* with certain tasks than He is the task itself. God knows that if we can't be faithful in "the little," we'll never be faithful with "the much." As it relates to supportive ministry, this passage in Luke teaches us to place value on what we are doing at the moment, even if we don't think it is what God has called us to do long-term. If we're not faithful in what we're doing right now, we will never get to where we want to go or do what we feel God has ultimately called us to do.

Sometimes people see what they are currently doing as a mere stepping-stone to something else–to the greener grass on the other side of the fence. People who take this point of view often give half-hearted effort and produce less-than-excellent results. Then, even if God has called them to something else, they are often not in a position to be promoted because they've not been faithful.

Martin Luther King Jr. conveyed the spirit of excellence we should all strive to attain when he said:

"If a man is called to be a streetsweeper, he should sweep streets even as Michelangelo painted or Beethoven composed music or Shakespeare wrote poetry. He should sweep streets so well that all the hosts of heaven and earth will pause to say 'Here lived a great streetsweeper who did his job well.'"[1]

Correction #2:
Be That Person!

I took the Lord's instruction on faithfulness to heart and began treating my job as though it were my ultimate calling and the most important thing I could ever do for God.

There was another time when my attitude needed an adjustment, and this time, the Lord spoke to my heart saying, "If *you* were the pastor, what kind of janitor would you want working for *you*?" It was easy to make a mental list; after all, if I were in charge, I would have high expectations of those working for me. After making the list, I sensed the Spirit say, "*You* be that janitor!"

> I WAS DOING MY JOB EXTERNALLY, BUT I WAS GRUMBLING INTERNALLY.

The immediate change in my feelings shocked me! It was easy for me to expect a high level of performance from a person I envisioned working *for me*, but it was much more challenging to measure up to that same standard when I was the one on the serving end of the equation. This challenge makes me mindful of what is commonly called "The Golden Rule."

MATTHEW 7:12 (*Message*)
12 Here is a simple, rule-of-thumb guide for behavior: Ask yourself what you want people to do for you, then grab the initiative and do it for them. Add up God's Law and Prophets and this is what you get.

In light of Matthew 7:12, I changed my attitude and worked to become the kind of janitor I would have wanted if I were the pastor. I obeyed the Word and "did unto others as I would have them do unto me."

Correction #3:
Do Your Work as Unto the Lord

Even though I corrected myself for a season when I received the first two admonitions, there was another time I let my attitude slip. I was doing my job *externally*, but I was grumbling *internally*. I remember standing in one of the restrooms cleaning the mirror and hearing the Holy Spirit speak to my heart, "Clean this restroom as though Jesus Himself were the next person coming in here." I realized at that moment that I had not been doing my work as unto the Lord.

COLOSSIANS 3:22–24 (*Message*)
22 **Servants, do what you're told by your earthly masters. And don't just do the minimum that will get you by. Do your best.**
23 **Work from the heart for your real Master, for God,**
24 **confident that you'll get paid in full when you come into your inheritance. Keep in mind always that the ultimate Master you're serving is Christ.**

To determine whether or not you are heeding the admonition of Colossians 3:22–24, ask yourself the following questions: What do you do when your pastor or supervisor walks in while you're working? Do you begin to work harder and more efficiently? Do you start being more polite or courteous? If so, why did you change the way you were working when a human authority figure walked in the room? Had you been working unto the Lord, you would have already been giving your very best whether or not another person was watching.

Correction can be hard on the flesh when it comes, but it produces great results when it is heeded (Heb. 12:11). I'm thankful that God helped me to correct my attitude. God wants us to have an attitude of commitment and excellence toward all our work. He wants us to serve others the way we would want to be served. And He wants us to do everything we do as unto Him.

QUESTIONS FOR REFLECTION AND DISCUSSION

1. Are you placing value on your current work for the Lord, or are you looking at what you're doing as a mere stepping-stone to something else?
2. Give some examples of the way you serve others according to how you want to be served.
3. Give some examples of how you do your work as unto the Lord instead of as unto men.
4. How do you typically respond to correction?
5. Has the Holy Spirit ever spoken a word of correction to you about your attitude or your performance? What changes did you make?
6. Is there anything of a corrective nature that God has brought to your attention recently? What are you going to do about it?
7. What did you learn from this chapter and how can you apply it?
8. What areas do you need to pray about or improve in?

---

[1] Reprinted, with permission of the publisher, from *Great Quotes from Great Leaders* " 1997 The Career Press Inc. Published by Career Press, Franklin Lakes, NJ. All rights reserved.

Four Commitments Supportive Ministers Must Make

In the previous chapter, I related three lessons I learned early in ministry through the Lord's correction. Those weren't the only lessons I learned or the only times I've been corrected. Growth is a process—and the process takes time.

People don't evolve into great staff members by accident, and supportive ministers aren't successful just because they show up for work. People must gradually develop and grow into great supportive ministers, and can only do so after first making and carrying out strong commitments in four essential areas:

1. Supportive ministers must be devoted to Jesus and to God's Word.
2. Supportive ministers must be devoted to the Church, or the Body of Christ.
3. Supportive ministers must be devoted to their own calling.
4. Supportive ministers must be devoted to the pastor for whom they work.

Commitment #1:
Devoted to God and His Word

Throughout the course of our ministry service, we must remember that before we became *fellow-workers* with God we were *children* of God. It may be difficult at times to separate the two relationships, but we must never forget that they are two separate roles. Many times people get so heavily involved in church work that they forget that the pre-eminent issue in life is having a personal relationship with Jesus. After commending the Ephesian church for certain positive traits, Jesus told them, *"Nevertheless I have this against you, that you have left your first love"* (Rev. 2:4). Remember, ministry work is not a substitute for a vibrant relationship with the Lord.

Mark 3:14–15 says, *"Then He* [Jesus] *appointed twelve, THAT THEY MIGHT BE WITH HIM and that He might send them out to preach, and to have power to heal sicknesses and to cast out demons."* Jesus' initial and top priority for the disciples was not for them to preach, but *"that they might be with Him."*

Jesus was not interested merely in the disciples' ministry productivity; He was deeply interested in their personal development and transformation of character. Furthermore, it was the disciples' character (formed and fashioned through their interaction with Jesus) that enabled them to truly be productive in ministry. How can we accurately represent Jesus if we don't know Him?

I once heard a minister say, "Some people, in the process of becoming great preachers, become lousy Christians." Some ministers have highly developed their preaching and ministry skills, but

> PERSONAL SPIRITUALITY AND GODLY CHARACTER SHOULD NEVER BE SACRIFICED ON THE ALTAR OF CHRISTIAN SERVICE.

have allowed their integrity, character, and, in some cases, even their morality to deteriorate. Personal spirituality and godly character should never be sacrificed on the altar of Christian service. Nor should one's position within the church lead to pride and cause him to lose his humility and holiness. A position or title in the church is never a substitute for personal spiritual growth.

Commitment #2:
Devoted to the Church

Those who love the Lord should also love His people and hold them in the highest regard. People who excel in supportive ministry embrace the truth that the Church—the Body of Christ—is vital, valuable, and precious to the Lord. Jesus loves the Church (Eph. 5:25), and so should we. Jesus is devoted to building His Church (Matt. 16:18), and if we love Jesus, then we must be committed to the same things to which He is committed.

We need to love the Church more than we love our position and more than we love the prestige or self-esteem that we draw from being in that position. This love is not a mere feeling, but should translate into positive actions such as faithful attendance, diligent service, and consistent financial support. These are some of the key characteristics that pastors look for *before* selecting people to serve in key positions in the church, and these character traits should continue after a person has stepped into leadership. These traits should not based on holding a formal position, but because of a person's love for and commitment toward Jesus' Church.

When a minister has a shepherd's heart, he will always consider the good of the Church in his decisions and actions. He will not do things that cause damage to the Church. A supportive minister should always seek the welfare and the well-being of the Church, just as Jesus does.

Commitment #3:
Devoted to Your Own Calling

Supportive ministry is more than a job—it's a calling. It is real ministry. Associate pastors, youth ministers, children's ministers, worship leaders, and others will sometimes receive such questions as, "When are you really going to go into ministry?" The implication is that only senior pastors are really in ministry. This is simply not true!

One staff minister I know went to visit someone in the hospital and was asked if "a *real* pastor" could come and visit. Supportive ministry *is* real and valid ministry and shouldn't be viewed as merely a stepping-stone to some other "nobler" venture. Supportive ministry is a noble venture in and of itself.

Realizing that you are called by God to supportive ministry adds value to what you do for Him and serves as an anchor of stability in difficult times. Knowing that the Lord has called you to serve and support enables you to view your assignment as a sacred trust to be carried out with all diligence and faithfulness. This sense of calling should motivate you to develop a high level of competence in your work and to perform your duties with excellence.

How a person is called isn't the issue. It's not a matter of how dramatic or how sensational the call is. For many, being "called" is more a growing awareness than a single dramatic event. The calling is often revealed in a God-given desire to serve the Lord and people, as well as in the presence of gifts and abilities that are needed for Kingdom work.

As a supportive minister, you need to know that God Himself and His calling are the ultimate reasons why you're doing what you're doing and that you will ultimately answer to God for how you perform your duties as a staff member or minister in the local church. You must always be mindful that being called by God is an honor, and He is the One Who will ultimately reward you for your service.

Commitment #4:
Devoted to the Pastor

Because the work of a supportive minister comes under the umbrella of the pastor's oversight of the local church, the supportive minister must work in harmony with the pastor, while always maintaining a submissive and respectful attitude. If we are committed to Jesus and His Church, then we need to be committed to the person He has placed in a position of leadership and authority within the local congregation.

Can you imagine an athlete saying the following? "I love the game of basketball; I am committed to the guys on my team; and I'm doing all I can to develop and improve my own skills. But I have no intention of cooperating with or respecting the coach of this team." On a practical level, that athlete will never excel or be productive on that team. His professed commitments sound great, but if he isn't willing to work with the coach and respect his authority, he is not going to be an asset to the team.

Successful supportive ministers—those who serve the way Timothy did—don't happen overnight. Growth takes time, patience, and commitment. Become devoted to God, His Church, your calling, and the pastor, and you will be further along the road to successful ministry.

QUESTIONS FOR REFLECTION AND DISCUSSION

1. How are you doing in your personal relationship with Jesus?
2. Has your work for the Lord caused you to lose any closeness to Him in terms of personal relationship?
3. How is your prayer life? Your Bible reading?
4. How is your commitment to the church? How would your commitment to the church change if you weren't working there in any capacity?
5. Do your church attendance, giving, and working come from your heart, or are you going through the motions?
6. Is your calling still fresh and vibrant to you?
7. Are you walking in the awareness of the fact that God called you to serve Him, or has your work become routine?
8. Are you mindful of the fact that you will ultimately answer to God for how you serve?

9. Do you view your work for the Lord in the context of teamwork? How are you showing proper respect and commitment toward the "coach"?
10. What did you learn from this chapter and how can you apply it?
11. What areas do you need to pray about or improve in?

Keeping Perspective by Keeping Priorities

In the previous two chapters, we've studied the *core values* and *commitments* necessary to be successful in supportive ministry. There are also some important *priorities* that a supportive minister must have in order to keep a proper perspective. We are going to study three of these priorities in this chapter: *first*, serve the purpose of God; *second*, respect the office in which the pastor stands; and, *third*, learn to work with the pastor's personality. Following these priorities and keeping them in their correct order will enable you to maintain perspective as you carry out the work of the ministry.

Priority One:
Serve the Purpose of God

Purpose transcends personality. It is important for supportive ministers to serve based on their awareness of God's purpose. His purpose is foundational and will remain steady when personality conflicts and other difficulties arise. Some people become enamored with the personality and charisma of a leader, and they begin working for that pastor based merely upon an attraction to a personality. It's great to like the people you work with and for, but ministry relationships that are only personality-based can be superficial and need to be built upon something stronger.

Challenges come to all types of relationships. Only the relationships that are built on a strong foundation will survive and thrive. For example, if someone marries only because of a personality attraction, what will happen when disagreements and conflicts arise? The Apostle Paul said that people who get married *"will have trouble in the flesh"* (1 Cor. 7:28). Paul wasn't being negative or pessimistic— just realistic. Trouble comes to every marriage. What the relationship is founded upon will determine whether or not it will outlast the trouble.

> KEEP IN MIND THAT YOU'RE NOT THE ONLY ONE HAVING TO "GET ALONG"; YOUR BOSS AND COWORKERS HAVE TO GET ALONG WITH YOU AND YOUR IMPERFECTIONS!

Picture a couple that said, "We occasionally see things differently and get frustrated with each other, but our marriage is not based on each other's personality. Our marriage is based on our commitment to God's intentions for us. We've discovered that love is not a euphoric feeling of infatuation, but it's a decision whereby we see one another and treat one another as valuable and precious—no matter what. We've chosen to honor and respect each other *even* when we disagree about something. Our commitment to marriage, based on God's purpose, is not shaken when we experience some friction caused by a personality difference or because one of us wasn't our best at a given time."

Imagine if this example of an attitude within marriage was the attitude shared by those working in the local church. A *principle*-based and *purpose*-based relationship will be strong and enduring, but a relationship that is merely *personality*-based is fragile and may not withstand life's inevitable challenges and pressures.

Priority Two:
Respect the Office in Which the Pastor Stands

Occasionally, a person chooses to join the staff of a pastor with whom they've been good friends for many years. While this may sound like a great arrangement, it has some potential downfalls. What happens the first time the pastor needs to function as "the boss" (and not as the friend) and needs to correct the supportive minister? Can the supportive minister step out of the friendship relationship and accept the correction—as coming from the pastor and not from a buddy?

People often have difficulty relating to the same person on two different levels because they can't separate the two roles in their thinking. The *friend* side of the relationship can cause a person to lose sight of the *pastoral office* and to not show appropriate respect. Regardless of whether or not there has been a long-standing friendship, any excessive sense of familiarity with the staff can undermine a leader's effectiveness.

> CHALLENGES COME TO ALL TYPES OF RELATIONSHIPS. ONLY THE RELATIONSHIPS THAT ARE BUILT ON A STRONG FOUNDATION WILL SURVIVE AND THRIVE.

When Jesus visited His hometown area, the people focused on Him from a standpoint of human familiarity instead of respecting the assignment God had given Him and the office (or position) in which He stood. The people said, *"Is this not the carpenter, the Son of Mary, and brother of James, Joses, Judas, and Simon? And are not His sisters here with us?"* (Mark 6:3). The verse goes on to say that the people were offended at Jesus.

The people in Jesus' hometown focused on who Jesus was in the natural instead of respecting the anointing upon His life. Because of their familiarity and subsequent lack of respect and faith, Jesus *"could do no mighty work there, except that He laid His hands on a few sick people and healed them"* (Mark 6:5). Jesus was not totally unable to minister, but His success was at a much lower level than what God desired because the people did not respect Jesus' office and were offended by Him.

An Extreme Example

In the Old Testament, David demonstrated tremendous respect for the office of the king even when King Saul behaved badly in that office. Even after Saul threw spears at David in effort to kill him, David still referred to Saul as "the Lord's anointed" and showed respect for the office in which Saul stood (1 Sam. 24:6,10; 26:9,11,16,23). Should Saul have dignified his office with better behavior? Certainly! But David was determined to act properly and do the right thing whether Saul did or not–even if it meant fleeing for his life! Determine in your heart that *you* will maintain the priority of respecting the offices God has established.

Priority Three:
Learn to Work With the Pastor's Personality

Although this priority is listed third, it may be the most difficult for some people to master. But there is a reason why it's listed third. If learning to work with a pastor's personality seems like a significant challenge, remember that keeping priorities one and two will enable you to meet that challenge with success.

The bottom line is, people have varying styles and personalities. If we are going to be successful in supportive ministry, we need to learn to work with the unique leadership style and personality of the pastor for whom we work. Every *leadership style* has its own strengths and weaknesses, and every *personality* has flaws and imperfections–no matter what type it is. Therefore, we need to exercise long-suffering patience and tolerance, not just for the pastor *for whom* we work, but also for the other people *with whom* we work. Keep in mind that you're not the only one having to "get along"; your boss and coworkers have to get along with you and your imperfections!

Ephesians 4:2–3 says, "Be humble and gentle. Be patient with each other, making allowance for each other's faults because of your love. Always keep yourselves united in the Holy Spirit, and bind yourselves together with peace" (*NLT*). Verse 2 in the *New King James Version* says we should be *"bearing with one another in love."* And the *Message* version of verse 3 says that we need to be "alert at noticing differences and quick at mending fences."

Bear With One Another

What does it mean to "bear with one another"? Commentators have offered the following thoughts:

- Bearing patiently with the foibles, faults, and infirmities of others.[1]
- A husband and wife—such is the imperfection of human nature—can find enough in each other to embitter life, if they choose to magnify imperfections, and to become irritated at trifles; and there is no friendship that may not be marred in this way, if we will allow it. Hence, if we would have life move on smoothly, we must learn to bear and forbear.[2]
- "...it may mean that, through the love of God working in our hearts, we should bear with each other's infirmities, ignorance, etc., knowing how much others have been or are still obliged to bear with us."[3]

A great example of bearing with one another (of making allowances for each other's faults) is found in the way Paul worked with Timothy. As we've seen, Timothy was an outstanding young man, but, like everyone else, he had areas of his life where he wasn't perfect.

(Keep in mind that if God waited until we were perfect before He allowed us to be in His service, none of us could ever serve. We shouldn't use this truth as a cop-out to not change or improve, but to encourage us to keep striving when we're tempted to quit, remembering we've all got room to grow.)

Timothy had a tendency to be intimidated (1 Tim. 4:12) and to pull back because of fear (2 Tim. 1:6–8). Paul encouraged Timothy in these matters on a personal level, but Paul also worked to create situations that were conducive to Timothy's success. For instance, Paul told the Corinthian church, *"If Timothy comes, see that he may be with you without fear; for he does the work of the Lord, as I also do. Therefore let no one despise him. But send him on his journey in peace..."* (1 Cor. 16:10–11).

Paul instructed believers to bear with one another, but Paul also practiced what he preached! He made allowances for Timothy's faults because of his love for the young minister.

If we are going to be strong supportive ministers, we must keep our perspective by maintaining proper priorities. Our top priority must be to serve the purpose of God, not a person or personality. Second, we must respect the office in which the pastor and other leaders stand. Third, we must learn to adapt to and flow with the pastor's personality and with the person-alities of others with whom we work. If we can successfully maintain these priorities, we can be successful in ministry.

QUESTIONS FOR REFLECTION AND DISCUSSION

1. Are you serving the purpose of God in what you are doing? What steps do you take to keep your focus on the purpose of God and not on people?
2. Do you respect the office of the pastor and the position of other leaders?
3. How do you keep yourself from slipping into areas of excessive familiarity?
4. Do you believe that you work well with the leadership style and the personality of your pastor and/or supervisor?
5. Are your expectations of others reasonable? Do you find yourself being overly-critical or perfectionistic in your expectations?
6. What is an appropriate and godly way to make allowances for other people's faults?

7. What did you learn from this chapter and how can you apply it?
8. What areas do you need to pray about or improve in?

---

[1] Albert Barnes, *Barnes' Notes on the New Testament* (Grand Rapids: Kregel, 1962), 991.

[2] Ibid., 991.

[3] Ralph Earle, ed., *Adam Clarke's Commentary on the Bible* (Grand Rapids: Baker Book House, 1967), 1179.

PART II

Biblical Examples of Supportive Ministry

In Part I, we studied various biblical principles of supportive ministry, and I illustrated these principles with examples from God's Word and from my personal ministerial experience and observations. But it is always helpful to study the lives of people who put these principles into practice—or *didn't*—and to see the results that come from choosing or refusing to apply these principles.

Therefore, in Part II of this book, we will take an in-depth look at the lives of various people throughout Bible history. Each chapter, we will focus on a particular leader and his supportive team and see how well they worked and served together. With each supportive minister, we will study their positive (and, in some cases, negative) traits and habits so you can learn from them both what *to do* and what *not to do* as you increase your value as a supportive minister by becoming more like Timothy everyday.

Paul and Timothy: Kindred Spirits

In Philippians chapter 2, Paul said he didn't have anyone who was like-minded except for Timothy.

PHILIPPIANS 2:19–22

19 But I trust in the Lord Jesus to send Timothy to you shortly, that I also may be encouraged when I know your state.

20 For I have no one like-minded, who will sincerely care for your state.

21 For all seek their own, not the things which are of Christ Jesus.

22 But you know his proven character, that as a son with his father he served with me in the gospel.

PHILIPPIANS 2:20–21 (*Amplified*)

20 For I have no one like him [no one of so kindred a spirit] who will be so genuinely interested in your welfare and devoted to your interests.

21 For the others all seek [to advance] their own interests, not those of Jesus Christ (the Messiah).

Timothy and Paul were like-minded and possessed a kindred spirit. The term "like-minded" comes from two Greek words that mean *equal soul*.[1]

Timothy knew and shared Paul's heart toward the Philippian believers and toward ministry in general. Timothy was the only one who thought the way Paul thought and who so mutually shared his values, priorities, purpose, convictions, and attitudes.

Why the Shortage of Good Help?

COULDN'T PAUL HAVE JUST CONDUCTED A CLASS ON "THE TWELVE PRINCIPLES OF LEADERSHIP" AND PRODUCED MORE TIMOTHYS?

Why did Paul only have one person who was like-minded? Didn't Paul want and need more? After all, wasn't he trying to minister to multiple congregations in various locations? Couldn't Paul have just conducted a class on "The Twelve Principles of Leadership" and produced more Timothys?

There is no doubt that Paul was a great leader, but even great leaders can't produce great followers without the cooperation and consent of the followers! As previously mentioned, great leadership doesn't produce optimum results without great follower-ship! If it had been up to Paul, he would have generated dozens of Timothys. If it had been up to God, I'm sure God would have wanted Paul to be surrounded by many talented, like-minded supportive ministers as well. So why only one?

Paul indicated that it was Timothy's own attitude that set him apart and put him in a class by himself. Paul himself said the reason he didn't have anyone else like-minded was because *"all seek their own"* (Phil. 2:21).

Some serving in ministry today are also "seeking their own." And this is a factor in the sense of alone-ness that leaders often face. Many are so caught up in their own life and personal pursuits that they fail to recognize the assignment or vision God has put within a pastor's heart. As a result, a pastor may have a large and compelling vision from God, but there may be few people willing to help bring that vision to pass. Why? They have their own vision to bring to pass!

Staff members and other leaders can have personal and conflicting agendas which cause them to seek their own good instead of the good of the team. Timothy offered something to Paul even more important than *ability*—he offered Paul his *availability*. All of the ability in the world is of no meaning if there's not also availability. I don't mean just physical availability; I'm referring to emotional, mental, and spiritual availability as well. Timothy was not self-promoting or self-willed, and he had no personal agenda; that's what made him so valuable and important to Paul. How tragic that Timothy's attitude was an exception when it should have been the norm!

Paul went on to say that Timothy had served with him as a son serves with a father. This speaks of the loyalty, devotion, and respect that Timothy had in his heart toward Paul. Timothy exercised ministry and leadership toward others in the context of serving and following Paul. He shared Paul's heart. He was like-minded.

A vital truth we see often in Scripture is that this Paul-and-Timothy-type of relationship was not merely functional or professional in nature. There was a knitting together of hearts. There was a divine connection—a God-birthed unity—whereby the people worked together for the plan and purpose of God to be furthered and fulfilled.

Paul's Trust in Timothy

Paul was in prison when he spoke of sending Timothy to the Philippians. People in prison are very restricted and limited, not able to go where they want to go or do what they want to do. It was from this confinement that Paul said, *"I trust in the Lord Jesus to send Timothy to you shortly"* (Phil. 2:19).

There are some rich truths in this passage from Philippians chapter 2. First, we see that Paul not only trusted in Jesus, but he had confidence in Timothy as well. Paul knew that Timothy would not drop the ball, so to speak, and that he would not misrepresent or undermine Paul in any way. Paul was not only persuaded of Timothy's ability to convey Paul's heart to the Philippians and to minister effectively to them, but Paul also knew that Timothy would bring him an accurate report concerning the condition of the Church in Philippi.

Paul trusted Timothy to be accountable, and Timothy's own sense of accountability to Paul was vital. Timothy was not being sent to Philippi to carry out his own agenda or to do his own thing. He was going to represent Paul and then to bring an accurate report back to Paul. Had Timothy been a self-willed, self-seeking, self-promoting type of person, he would have exploited Paul's limitations and restrictions. He would have used the occasion of Paul's imprisonment to strengthen his personal agenda and to create a following for himself.

One of Timothy's outstanding characteristics is that he didn't see Paul's limitations as an opportunity to be seized upon for self-gain; he merely added value to Paul by becoming an extension of Paul's ministry to the Philippians. Men of lesser character might have presented themselves as a *substitute* for Paul instead of as an *extension* of Paul. What set Timothy apart was his loyalty and heart-connection to his father in the faith.

Not only did Paul say that Timothy was like-minded to himself, but he also told the Philippians that Timothy *"will sincerely care for your state"* (Phil. 2:20). Timothy was no hireling; his heart was totally involved in what he did. Seeking the things of Jesus Christ and serving Paul were woven into the very fabric of his being. He shared Paul's heart to the point that Paul said, *"As a son with his father he served with me in the gospel"* (Phil. 2:22).

The Need for Modern-Day Timothys

How does all of this relate to us? Every pastor today is limited and restricted by the mere fact that he is a human being. Though he is anointed by God, the pastor is confined to one physical body—he can only be in one place at one time—and has limited time and talents. No pastor (or any other member of the Body of Christ) possesses all gifts and abilities or has an infinite measure of the Holy Spirit. The Bible teaches that the Lord Jesus Christ had the Spirit "without measure or limit" (John 3:34 *NLT*), but the

> To say that each of us is *DEFICIENT BY DESIGN* IS NOT A CRITICISM OR AN INSULT, BUT IS A REALISTIC AND HONEST ADMISSION THAT GOD DID NOT GIVE ANY ONE PERSON ALL THE SPIRITUAL GIFTS.

rest of us have *"gifts differing according to the grace that is given to us"* (Rom. 12:6).

Jesus operated in the fullness of every spiritual gift, ability, and anointing. He was the ultimate apostle, the ultimate prophet, the ultimate evangelist, the ultimate pastor, and the ultimate teacher. There was no gift or ability that He didn't have. Jesus is the only One Who has ever operated in that capacity. Every pastor and believer today is what we might call "deficient by design."

Deficient by Design

To say that each of us is *deficient by design* is not a criticism or an insult, but is a realistic and honest admission that God did not give any one person all the spiritual gifts. In other words, God didn't put all His eggs in one basket! In His infinite wisdom, God did not give me or anyone else (individually) all the gifts necessary for ministry in the Body of Christ. If I had every single gift necessary, then I could begin to believe that I didn't need other people.

God deliberately made me deficient. The gifts He didn't give to me, He may have given to you. The gifts He didn't give to you or me, He gave to someone else. The only way the local church can be successful is for us to first recognize that we are individually deficient by design, then to honor and respect the gifts He's given others, and finally to use them together—in partnership and teamwork—for the building up of the Kingdom.

This does not undermine the pastor's authority or minimize his role of leadership, but simply highlights the fact that we all need each other. Just like Paul needed Timothy to go places in his stead and to interact with people he could not personally reach, pastors today are in need of Timothys who will represent them and function in different capacities and, at the same time, be accountable in their work.

The unity that Paul and Timothy walked in does not infer that they had identical personalities. On the contrary, in studying the Word of God closely, it becomes evident that Paul and Timothy had very different personalities. Paul had an extremely strong personality. He saw most issues in black and white, with no gray areas. Paul was dogmatic, opinionated, and strong. Timothy, on the other hand, struggled with inferiority. He had a tendency to be intimidated by others and had to deal with fear. Though Paul and Timothy had very different *personalities*, Paul still said that Timothy was *like-minded*, or of equal soul.

My prayer for the Body of Christ today is that there will arise a generation of supportive ministers who will not have merely a professional, formal relationship with their pastors, but will become true spiritual Timothys—supportive ministers who will be like-minded, who will sincerely care for the people, and who will walk in true partnership with the senior pastor. May every church leadership team walk together in unity and work together in harmony.

QUESTIONS FOR REFLECTION AND DISCUSSION

1. In what ways am I like-minded to my pastor?
2. Do I know my pastor's values? Priorities? Convictions? What are they? Do I share them?
3. What made Timothy different from the others? What put him a class by himself?
4. What does the phrase "deficient by design" mean?
5. Have you ever become critical of a leader and found fault with his shortcomings?

6. When you see your pastor's limitations and restrictions, do you recognize those limits and restrictions as normal, then seek to add value to him by being an extension of his ministry?
7. What did you learn from this chapter and how can you apply it?
8. What areas do you need to pray about or improve in?

---

[1] W.E. Vine, *An Expository Dictionary of New Testament Words*, Volume II (Old Tappan, NJ: Fleming H. Revell Company, 1940), 343.

Paul and Mark:
If at First You Don't
Succeed...

While Timothy was very special to Paul, there were other people who also helped Paul at different times in his ministry. I want to study a few of them in the next two chapters.

The first person I want to look at is Mark. Second Timothy 4:11 shows how much Paul esteemed Mark's help in the ministry.

2 Timothy 4:11
11 ...Get Mark and bring him with you, FOR HE IS USEFUL TO ME FOR MINISTRY.

2 Timothy 4:11 (*KJV*)
11 ...Take Mark, and bring him with thee: FOR HE IS PROFITABLE TO ME FOR THE MINISTRY.

2 Timothy 4:11 (*Message*)
11 ...Bring Mark with you; HE'LL BE MY RIGHT-HAND MAN.

Second Timothy 4:11 reveals that Paul saw great value in Mark and his ministry. But Paul had not always considered Mark a ministerial asset. In fact, there was a time when Paul thought of Mark as an unnecessary *liability*.

Liability or Asset?

Paul and Barnabas took Mark with them on their first missionary journey, but he did not complete the journey with them. Acts 13:13 in the *Message* says, "From Paphos, Paul and company put out to sea, sailing on to Perga in Pamphylia. That's where [Mark] called it quits and went back to Jerusalem."

When Paul and Barnabas were going to back to check on the churches later, Barnabas wanted to give Mark a second chance, but Paul was unwilling to do so (see Acts 15:36–41). The dispute over Mark was so volatile that Paul and Barnabas split company—Paul chose Silas and resumed the missionary work, while Barnabas took young Mark with him and went to Cyprus.

We don't know all that happened concerning Mark's development, but we do know that Barnabas must have nurtured him and worked with him through a potentially devastating experience. Many young ministers would have quit the ministry forever had they experienced failure and rejection of that magnitude. But Barnabas was determined to not let that happen to Mark. True to the meaning of his name, Barnabas ("The Son of Encouragement") stepped into this struggling young minister's life, believed in his potential, and cultivated the gift that was within him.

Once Unprofitable—Now Profitable

THE NECESSARY TRAITS TO BEING PROFITABLE FOR MINISTRY CAN BE CULTIVATED, AND PEOPLE CAN GO FROM BEING UNPROFITABLE TO BEING PROFITABLE.

What can we learn from Mark's experience? First, if we miss it and seem unprofitable for ministry, there is hope for growth and eventual restoration. Second, we may be called upon to be a Barnabas—to graciously minister restoration and encouragement to a fallen minister.

There may be people who at times are not profitable to the ministry. There may be times when certain people are not profitable to their pastor because of immaturities, insecurities, or attitude issues. But becoming profitable is a skill that can be learned and developed. The necessary traits to being profitable for ministry can be cultivated, and people can go from being unprofitable to being profitable.

For Paul to have called for Mark those many years later may possibly indicate some mellowing on Paul's part. But Paul certainly saw the changes and maturity that had taken place in Mark. Had Mark not grown in grace, he probably would have harbored resentment toward Paul. Upon hearing Paul's request for his company, Mark could have thought, *When I needed you to give me a break, you wouldn't show any mercy. Now you're in prison and you need me, but I no longer need you.* But we are confident that no such attitude existed in Mark. Rather, his spiritual maturity had truly positioned him to be *profitable for the ministry.*

A Prayer for Supportive Ministers

When I first began in supportive ministry, I realized that like Timothy, I, too, was a young minister, and I also needed the mentoring of a seasoned, mature minister—someone who knew the ropes and could teach them to me. Who better to learn from than the Apostle Paul? So I read First and Second Timothy over and over again. The very purpose of these pastoral epistles to Timothy was, *"So that you may know how you ought to conduct yourself in the house of God, which is the church of the living God, the pillar and ground of the truth"* (1 Tim. 3:15).

One of the things that stood out to me in Second Timothy was the verse where the great apostle told Timothy to bring Mark with him, because Mark would be profitable to Paul for the ministry. That really struck a chord with me, and it became the basis for a prayer that I prayed often: "Lord, make me profitable—beneficial and useful—to the man of God for whom I work."

I encourage you to make that your prayer as well as you strive by the grace of God to become a profitable asset in the ministry.

QUESTIONS FOR REFLECTION AND DISCUSSION

1. Have you ever messed up and caused yourself to seem unprofitable for the ministry? What did you do to restore yourself to a position of being profitable?
2. What did you do to regain the trust of those in positions of spiritual leadership?
3. Can your pastor say of you what Paul said of Mark: "He is profitable to me for the ministry?" If so, why? If not, why not?
4. What can you do to make yourself more profitable, beneficial, and useful to your pastor for the work of the ministry?
5. What are any attitudes, traits, or characteristics you have right now that would make you more of a liability than an asset to your pastor?
6. Is there someone you know that you might need to be a Barnabas to? Is there someone who may have failed or is otherwise discouraged concerning ministry that you could encourage and nurture back into active service for the Lord?
7. What did you learn from this chapter and how can you apply it?
8. What areas do you need to pray about or improve in?

Paul and Others:
Strategic Connections

We've seen that Timothy helped Paul, as did Silas, Barnabas, and Mark. But whether or not other people supported him, Paul was fully committed to faithfully serving the Lord Jesus Christ. Paul said, *"At my first defense no one stood with me, but all forsook me. May it not be charged against them. But the Lord stood with me and strengthened me..."* (2 Tim. 4:16–17).

Even though Paul was willing to serve Jesus alone if people forsook him or weren't willing to join his cause, Paul preferred working in partnership with others—and did so whenever he could. Paul had needs just like everyone else, and he had a deep appreciation for those who ministered to him and encouraged him. Consider the heartfelt gratitude Paul expressed in the way he spoke of those who partnered with him and supported him throughout his ministry:

Titus:[1]
- Titus is a true son.
- God, who comforts the downcast, comforted us by the coming of Titus.
- Titus is my partner and fellow worker.
- Did Titus and I not walk in the same spirit? Did we not walk in the same steps?

Tychicus:[2]
- A beloved brother, faithful minister, and fellow servant in the Lord.
- Tychicus is my fellow worker for the Kingdom of God. He has proved to be a comfort to me.

Onesiphorus:[3]
- He often refreshed me and was not ashamed of my chain. He sought me out very zealously and found me. You know very well how many ways he ministered to me at Ephesus.

Prisca and Aquila:[4]
- My fellow workers in Christ Jesus, who risked their own necks for my life—to whom I give thanks.

Stephanas, Fortunatus, and Achaicus:[5]
- What was lacking on your part they supplied. They refreshed my spirit.

Epaphroditus:[6]
- My brother, fellow worker, and fellow soldier—the one who ministered to my need.

Unnamed Believers:[7]
- "And so we came to Rome. And the [Christian] brethren there, having had news of us, came as far as the Forum of Appius and the three Taverns to meet us. When Paul saw them, he thanked God and received new courage."

You can sense the joy, comfort, and strength that Paul received from the help, support, and friendship of these fellow workers and friends. Though there were times when Paul felt alone-ness in working for God, there were certainly other times when Paul experienced the warmth of companionship and partnership in ministry.

These aforementioned relationships reflected the truth of Proverbs 25:13, which says, *"Like the cold of snow in time of harvest is a faithful messenger to those who send him, for he refreshes the soul of his masters."* This truth can be the basis for another prayer by those who serve in supportive ministry: "Lord, may my faithfulness and the way I conduct myself be a source of joy, refreshing, and strength to those *for whom* and *with whom* I work."

The Meaning and Value of Synergy

The Greek word that Paul used to describe his partnership with Timothy, Titus, and others was "sunergos," which is translated *fellow worker* or *fellow laborer*.[8] This is where we get the word "synergy" today. Synergy is a word used to describe the effect of two different components or people coming together to accomplish something that neither of them could have accomplished alone.

> SYNERGY IS A WORD USED TO DESCRIBE THE EFFECT OF TWO DIFFERENT COMPONENTS OR PEOPLE COMING TOGETHER TO ACCOMPLISH SOMETHING THAT NEITHER OF THEM COULD HAVE ACCOMPLISHED ALONE.

One of the best illustrations of synergy is the chemical compound called H_2O, better known as *water*. Isolated, the element hydrogen is limited in what it can do, and the same is true for oxygen. But when these gases—hydrogen and oxygen—are joined together, water is produced! This "partnership" can accomplish things that neither hydrogen nor oxygen can accomplish on its own.

When Christians join together (whether it be staff members or church members), they produce results as a team that not one of them could have produced on his own. There is strength in the *Body* of Christ when each *part* of the Body works in conjunction with every other part.

In Ephesians chapter 4, the Apostle Paul addressed the growth, development, and maturing process of the Body of Christ. He mentions the different ministry gifts (apostles, prophets, evangelists, pastors, and teachers) and then refers to *"the whole body, joined and knit together by what every joint supplies, according to the effective working by which every part does its share..."* (Eph. 4:16).

Most pastors have preached messages about how important it is for every member of the Body of Christ to do his or her part. While that's important, it should be noted that before Paul mentions *"the effective working by which every part does its share,"* he uses the phrase *"joined and knit together by what every joint supplies."*

Strategic Connections

What is a joint? It is a strategic connection. It's one thing for every member to do his or her part, but if we're not joined together properly (if we don't have the right strategic connections), our individual efforts may be *dis*jointed and produce diminished results. If churches are going to rise to their potential, there must be more than individual parts functioning in isolated ways. There have to be joints, or strategic connections. The right people have to be in the right places, working together and using their specific gifts in a cooperative manner toward a common purpose.

In Ephesians chapter 4, Paul was not minimizing individual effort, because individual effort is important. But Paul is emphasizing that it's not just isolated, individual effort that will ultimately get the job done. People must come together and work together as fellow laborers. Then, and only then, will real synergy occur. According to Paul, working together is what generates a true supply of the spiritual nutrients that produce maturity, growth, and development in the Body of Christ.

Paul was refreshed, comforted, and encouraged by the strategic relationships in his life. They helped him function more effectively as a minister of the Gospel. He preferred working in partnerships because of the strength that those strategic relationships produced.

QUESTIONS FOR REFLECTION AND DISCUSSION

1. What did Paul do in his ministry when other people did not do the right thing—when they forsook him or failed to appreciate his ministry toward them? Did Paul ever quit, or did he persevere in fulfilling his ministry?

2. To what degree did Paul notice and appreciate it when others partnered with him and stood by his side as fellow workers in the ministry?
3. Paul mentioned people who ministered to him, comforted him, encouraged him, and refreshed him. How does your conduct provide that type of support to those for whom and with whom you work?
4. Are you doing your part in the Body of Christ? How are you strategically connected to others in working together for the maturing of the Body of Christ according to Ephesians 4:16? (*"From whom the whole body, joined and knit together by what every joint supplies, according to the effective working by which every part does its share, causes growth of the body for the edifying of itself in love."*)
5. What did you learn from this chapter and how can you apply it?
6. What areas do you need to pray about or improve in?

---

[1] Titus 1:4; 2 Corinthians 7:6; 8:23; 12:18

[2] Colossians 4:7–11

[3] 2 Timothy 1:16–18

[4] Romans 16:3–4

[5] 1 Corinthians 16:17–18

[6] Philippians 2:25

[7] Acts 28:14–15 (*Amplified*)

[8] W.E. Vine, *An Expository Dictionary of New Testament Words*, Volume IV (Old Tappan, NJ: Fleming H. Revell Company, 1940), 232.

Jesus and His Disciples

Very often in the Body of Christ God deliberately joins together people who have very different *spiritual giftings* and very different *personalities* as well. What a boring world this would be if we were all clones of each other! If everyone on a church leadership team had the same personality, it would be a very monotonous group. As a matter of fact, if any two of us were identical in every way, one of us would be unnecessary!

When Jesus put His team of twelve together it was an interesting mixture. Two of Jesus' disciples were zealots. Zealots were Jewish people who were passionate in their disdain for the Roman occupation of their land. Then Jesus recruited Matthew, a Jewish man who had sold out, so to speak, to the Roman occupiers by serving as one of their tax-collectors. Jesus couldn't have chosen three people who were on more opposite ends of the spectrum, and yet He put them on the same team and expected them to work together for a common cause.

Mark chapter 3 gives us insight into just what their common cause would be.

MARK 3:13–15

13 And He went up on the mountain and called to Him those He Himself wanted. And they came to Him.

14 Then He appointed twelve, that they might be with Him and that He might send them out to preach,

15 and to have power to heal sicknesses and to cast out demons.

One of the most overlooked aspects of the relationship that Jesus had with His twelve disciples has to do with the purpose and priorities of their calling. We often think only of the fact that Jesus called them so that they could preach and be leaders of the Church after His resurrection. However, their eventual preaching and ministry was actually a *secondary* issue, at least according to this passage of scripture in Mark chapter 3. The *initial* priority Jesus had for The Twelve was *"THAT THEY MIGHT BE WITH HIM"* (v. 14).

Information vs. Transformation

> THE VARIOUS FUNCTIONS THE DISCIPLES PERFORMED WERE IMPORTANT, BUT WHAT HAPPENED IN THEIR LIVES AS A RESULT OF THEIR RELATIONSHIP WITH JESUS WAS EVEN MORE IMPORTANT.

The various functions the disciples performed were important, but what happened in their lives as a result of their relationship with Jesus was even more important. What occurred *internally*, in their character, is what eventually enabled their *external* work to be truly reflective of Jesus.

Jesus knew that accumulation of information about God would not be sufficient; rather, the disciples needed to be inwardly transformed—and would be through their association with Him. *Information is important, but transformation is vital.* By being with Jesus, the disciples were able to absorb His values, priorities, and purpose. They were able to receive His mission as their own (John 20:21).

Jesus Chose the Ones He Wanted

Jesus, as the leader, had the prerogative to choose who His key people would be. This was not a matter of mere volunteerism (although volunteering does have its place). Mark 3:13 says, Jesus *"called to Him those He Himself wanted."* Part of Jesus' headship involved appointing those who would serve in the top leadership roles of His team.

The mentoring that Jesus provided His disciples focused on their development and transformation, and He taught them at a deeper level than He taught the multitudes. Jesus told the twelve, *"To you it has been given to know the mystery of the kingdom of God; but to those who are outside, all things come in parables"* (Mark 4:11). Jesus taught the multitudes using parables, but when He was alone with the disciples *"He explained all things"* (Mark 4:33-34).

Necessary Functions

In addition to making sure His disciples were *learning* and *becoming*, Jesus made sure they were also involved in *doing*. The disciples served Jesus by carrying out various tasks and by helping facilitate His ministry objectives. Often, they focused on practical tasks that not only helped Jesus' ministry, but also contributed to their own development as ministers. Consider some of the following jobs they performed:

- Following a day of Jesus' teaching, the disciples provided transportation for Jesus. They rowed while He slept (Mark 4:35-38).
- Jesus' disciples arranged accommodations for Him when He traveled. Luke 9:52 tells us that Jesus "sent messengers on ahead to make arrangements for his hospitality" (*Message*).
- Peter assisted Jesus in the paying of His taxes (Matt. 17:24-27).
- The disciples helped in organizational matters. When Jesus fed the multitude, He had the disciples seat the people in groups of fifty. Jesus performed the miracle of multiplying the loaves and fishes, and the disciples then served the people in groups (Luke 9:14-17).

- The disciples arranged transportation for Jesus' entry into Jerusalem (Matt. 21:1–3). They also made arrangements for and set up the Passover meal that Jesus shared with them (Luke 22:7–13).
- One of Jesus' staff members had been assigned the task of overseeing the ministry finances. John 13:29 says that Judas was their treasurer (*NLT*).

Why did Jesus have His disciples handle these tasks? Certainly, it was a part of their development and training. In this sense, we could say that the disciples were assigned the tasks *for their own good*—to teach and train them and assist in their development. But there is another reason Jesus delegated these duties—it was *for His good*. These were necessary duties, yet Jesus knew that it wasn't practical or expedient for *Him* to do them.

Please don't misunderstand me. Jesus didn't consider Himself above doing what others might consider "menial tasks." His washing the disciples' feet demonstrated that! But Jesus' assignment required that He focus on other things. He specialized in teaching, preaching, and healing (Matt. 9:35). Jesus allowed His disciples to take care of natural details so He could more effectively focus on the specific things that God had called *Him* to do.

Perhaps it was Jesus' delegation of these administrative issues that prompted these same apostles to later say, "*...It is not desirable that we should leave the word of God and serve tables. Therefore, brethren, seek out from among you seven men of good reputation, full of the Holy Spirit and wisdom, whom we may appoint over this business; but we will give ourselves continually to prayer and to the ministry of the word*" (Acts 6:2–4).

The men who had been with Jesus had learned from Jesus. As they *learned, became*, and *did* under Jesus' supervision, they were preparing and training for the day when Jesus would no longer be with them (in the flesh). All of their transformation and training equipped them to then carry out their future ministry assignments.

Malfunctions and Misrepresentations

The time the disciples spent with Jesus was invaluable. How would they ever accurately represent Jesus without spending time with Him? Learning to be like Jesus took time—and the disciples weren't transformed overnight.

Sometimes Jesus' disciples didn't behave the way He wanted them to behave. Instead of *representing* Him, they often *misrepresented* Him. Consider the following examples:

- James and John wanted to call down fire from heaven to destroy a Samaritan village that was unreceptive to Jesus (Luke 9:54–56).
- The disciples wanted to send away a woman who was seeking healing for her daughter, but Jesus healed the daughter (Matt. 15:21–28).
- The disciples wanted to send the multitudes away; Jesus desired to feed them (Matt. 14:13–21).
- The disciples went contrary to Jesus' desires when they rebuked those who had brought children to Jesus to be blessed. The disciples thought the children would bother Jesus, but He was pleased to bless them (Mark 10:13–16).

There were also times when the disciples (namely Peter) endeavored to lead when they should have been following. In one such instance, when Jesus explained to the disciples that he was to be killed in Jerusalem, Peter took Jesus aside and began to rebuke Him. Jesus responded by saying, *"Get behind Me, Satan! You are an offense to Me, for you are not mindful of the things of God, but the things of men"* (Matt. 16:23).

Consider also what happened on the Mount of Transfiguration where instead of following the agenda, Peter tried to dictate one:

LUKE 9:33–35 (*NLT*)

33 As Moses and Elijah were starting to leave, Peter, not even knowing what he was saying, blurted out, "Master, this is wonderful! We will make three

shrines—one for you, one for Moses, and one for
Elijah."

34 But even as he was saying this, a cloud came over
them; and terror gripped them as it covered them.

35 Then a voice from the cloud said, "This is my Son, my
Chosen One. Listen to him."

In an awe-inspiring way, God told Peter, "Now is the time
for you to follow, not the time to lead. Now is the time for
you to listen, not the time for you to talk" (v. 35). This is a lesson we need to learn as well. As supportive ministers, we will
have times to talk, but when the pastor or leader is talking—it's
time to listen!

Being With Jesus

In spite of the disciples' many flaws, mistakes, and shortcomings, Jesus loved them deeply. At the Last Supper, He told
them, *"BUT YOU ARE THOSE WHO HAVE CONTINUED WITH ME in
My trials. And I bestow upon you a kingdom, just as My Father
bestowed one upon Me"* (Luke 22:28–29). Jesus expressed His gratitude to the disciples for their being with Him for the past
three years. Jesus knew it hadn't always been easy, and He
thanked and rewarded the disciples for their faithful commitment to Him.

Later, the Sanhedrin recognized the fact that Peter and
John had been with Jesus and in doing so paid them what is
perhaps the ultimate compliment we can receive from another
person:

ACTS 4:13

13 Now when they saw the boldness of Peter and John,
and perceived that they were uneducated and
untrained men, they marveled. And they realized that
THEY HAD BEEN WITH JESUS.

What an awesome compliment for Peter and John—to have
the world recognize that they had been with Jesus. When *our*

thoughts, words, and actions become Christ-like, the people *we* meet will recognize that *we*, too, have been with Jesus—because it's only by spending time with Jesus that our thoughts, words, and actions will ever be transformed into His image.

Again, Mark 3:14 reveals that Jesus had a primary objective when He first called the disciples. He chose them *"THAT THEY MIGHT BE WITH HIM."* Through the inward transformation process that occurred during their intimate relationship with Jesus, the disciples were enabled to be His representatives and fellow-workers in the building of His Church. They had *learned*. They had *done*. And they had *become*.

QUESTIONS FOR REFLECTION AND DISCUSSION

1. On a scale of 1–10, how would you rate your development in terms of learning, doing, and becoming? List some evidence showing how you are growing in all three areas of knowledge, service, and character development.
2. To what degree have you taken hold of your pastor's vision and mission for your church? How have you embraced the vision/mission and made it your own?
3. What tasks (natural duties) does your pastor have to handle that someone else in the church could and should be doing?
4. Are you representing the vision of the pastor and the mission of the church or are you misrepresenting them? Are you "functioning" or "malfunctioning"?
5. What did you learn from this chapter and how can you apply it?
6. What areas do you need to pray about or improve in?

CHAPTER 10

John the Baptist: Promoting the Success of Another

They came to John and said, "Rabbi, you know the one who was with you on the other side of the Jordan? The one you authorized with your witness? Well, he's now competing with us. He's baptizing, too, and everyone's going to Him instead of us."

John answered, "It's not possible for a person to succeed— I'm talking about eternal success—without heaven's help.

You yourselves were there when I made it public that I was not the Messiah but simply the one sent ahead of him to get things ready.

The one who gets the bride is, by definition, the bridegroom. And the bridegroom's friend, his 'best man'—that's me—in place at his side where he can hear every word, is genuinely happy. How could he be jealous when he knows that the wedding is finished and the marriage is off to a good start? That's why my cup is running over.

This is the assigned moment for him to move into the center, while I slip off to the sidelines."

—John 3:26–30 (*Message*)

He must increase, but I must decrease.

–John 3:30

> JOHN THE BAPTIST REALIZED THAT "WE" IS MORE IMPORTANT THAN "ME."

John the Baptist was not territorial or defensive about his position, and he actually promoted Jesus in such a way as to encourage his own followers to transfer their loyalty to the Savior. In John's Gospel we read, *"Again, the next day, John stood with two of his disciples. And looking at Jesus as He walked, he said, 'Behold the Lamb of God!' The two disciples heard him speak, and they followed Jesus"* (John 1:35–37). John the Baptist did not use his ministry assignment to promote himself or to build a personal following; he was actually pleased that his efforts contributed to the success of another person's ministry.

Had John the Baptist been a man of lesser character, he could have been jealous when Jesus began to move into the spotlight. He could have thought, *Wait a minute. I'm older than Jesus. I've been in ministry longer than Jesus. I'm the one who introduced Jesus to the public. I promoted Him, and now people are looking to Him instead of to me.* John was willing to do the job God had assigned to him and was not bothered when Jesus began to receive more attention than he.

Though John the Baptist was never technically on Jesus' staff (in the way the twelve disciples were), he demonstrated a commendable attitude that all staff members and supportive ministers should strive to possess. John the Baptist realized that "we" is more important than "me."

'We' Is More Important Than 'Me'

John the Baptist had a Kingdom-mentality, not a self-mentality. He wanted what was best for the Kingdom, not necessarily what was best for him personally. Successful supportive ministers are willing to promote the leadership of the senior pastor and of others on the team. They avoid being competitive with other leaders, and they are not concerned about who gets the credit, who gets attention, and who is recognized. They care more about "we" than "me," and the good of the team is more important than their personal popularity, position, or prominence.

Far too often, people only have a mentality of self-preservation and self-promotion. Their top priority is revealed by their attitude, which says, "I'm going to defend my position and my popularity at all costs. It doesn't matter if the Kingdom could be better served if I were to let someone else advance."

John the Baptist demonstrated an attitude of deferring to another in a wonderful and powerful way. How could this godly attitude be applied in ministry today? Imagine a scenario in a church where someone has been playing the drums for a long time. He's a good drummer, and he's been faithful. However, a new person joins the church who is an outstanding drummer with considerably superior skills to the regular drummer. The newer person has now become a faithful member of the church, has demonstrated good character, and has a willingness to serve.

What should the regular drummer do? Does he feel threatened, defensive, and suspicious? Does he feel a need to discredit the new person out of fear of losing his position? Or does he tell the pastor, "I've been drumming here at the church for several years and have really enjoyed it. However, we now have a church member who possesses far better skills than I do. He can take our worship to a higher level. I'd like to ask that you give him my position, and I'll be glad to serve as the back-up drummer. In the meantime, I'd like to volunteer to work in other areas, so I can continue to help the church and develop other gifts in my life." Can you imagine such a scene ever taking place in *your* church?

There is a great scene in the movie "Remember the Titans" that illustrates this principle of deference beautifully. In the championship game, a defensive back for the Titan football team is sitting on the bench for disciplinary reasons. The substitute defensive back who is in the game realizes that he is unable to keep up with the receiver he has been assigned to defend. Because this substitute player cares more about the success of the team than he does about his own playing time, he goes to the coach and pleads for the regular defensive back to be put in the game. With the coach's permission, the substitute goes to the regular defensive back and tells him to take his place on the playing field. That act of selflessness on the part of the substitute defensive back was a key factor in the Titans' eventual victory.

Putting other people ahead of you can be hard on the flesh, but it exemplifies the kind of attitude that John the Baptist possessed. Whether it's allowing the pastor to shine or allowing another team member to advance, we need to be willing to decrease at times so that others–especially the entire team as a whole–can increase.

QUESTIONS FOR REFLECTION AND DISCUSSION

1. Do you rejoice when others are promoted, or do you feel jealous?
2. Is there someone in your church who has really exemplified the attitude of John the Baptist–someone who is happy to slip off to the sidelines while others move into the spotlight?
3. Are you willing to work behind the scenes to help make the pastor and the team look good, even if you're not necessarily the one getting the credit?
4. Would you be willing to serve in a different capacity than the one in which you are now serving if it would help your church to be more effective?
5. What did you learn from this chapter and how can you apply it?
6. What areas do you need to pray about or improve in?

Moses and Those Who Helped Him

We've studied several New Testament leaders and their supportive ministry teams. In the next few chapters, we will study some supportive ministry examples from the Old Testament, starting with Moses and those who helped him.

When Moses received the call of God to go and deliver the children of Israel from Egyptian bondage he was overwhelmed by the magnitude of the assignment. Consider some of his responses to God:

- *"Who am I that I should go to Pharaoh, and that I should bring the children of Israel out of Egypt?"* (Exod. 3:11).
- *"But suppose they will not believe me or listen to my voice; suppose they say, 'The Lord has not appeared to you'"* (Exod. 4:1).
- *"O my Lord, I am not eloquent, neither before nor since You have spoken to Your servant; but I am slow of speech and slow of tongue"* (Exod. 4:10).

Even though God told Moses that His divine Presence and power would ensure a successful mission, Moses went on to say, "Lord, please! Send someone else" (Exod. 4:13 *NLT*). God was not pleased with Moses' unbelief, but He assigned Moses' brother Aaron to help him carry out what he had been told to do. Aaron helped Moses throughout the course of Moses' ministry, and Moses also received assistance from many others.

Moses Learns to Rely on Others

We saw in chapter 2 that Moses had a tendency to be a "do-it-yourself" kind of guy. Through various situations and challenges, Moses learned to rely on others—and it saved his life and ministry. Consider the teamwork that was necessary in Israel's battle with the Amalekites:

EXODUS 17:9–13

9   And Moses said to Joshua, "Choose us some men and go out, fight with Amalek. Tomorrow I will stand on the top of the hill with the rod of God in my hand."

10   So Joshua did as Moses said to him, and fought with Amalek. And Moses, Aaron, and Hur went up to the top of the hill.

11   And so it was, when Moses held up his hand, that Israel prevailed; and when he let down his hand, Amalek prevailed.

12   But Moses' hands became heavy; so they took a stone and put it under him, and he sat on it. And Aaron and Hur supported his hands, one on one side, and the other on the other side; and his hands were steady until the going down of the sun.

13   So Joshua defeated Amalek and his people with the edge of the sword.

> JOSHUA COULD HAVE SAID, "WAIT A MINUTE. WHY DO *I* HAVE TO GO FIGHT THE AMALEKITES WHILE MOSES SITS AND WATCHES FROM THE HILLTOP?…"

Notice in this passage of scripture how everyone had his own part to play: Moses, Joshua, Aaron, Hur, and the entire army of Israel all functioned in different capacities, but they were striving for a common goal and purpose.

Joshua could have said, "Wait a minute. Why do *I* have to go fight the Amalekites while Moses sits and watches from the hilltop? Why am *I* doing all the hard work when *he's* the leader?" But Joshua didn't have this kind of attitude. He knew he had a job to do, and he did it with his whole heart. Joshua also knew that Moses had a job to do—a different kind of job—and he respected the role that Moses fulfilled. It could be said that Joshua did the "hands-on" work, but Moses did the "hands-up" work. Leaders today still need people to help hold up their hands!

Another example of teamwork is found in Exodus chapter 18. Jethro observed his son-in-law Moses trying to single-handedly solve everyone's problems. This prompted Jethro to give Moses some wise counsel concerning the need and benefit of delegation and teamwork.

EXODUS 18:19–23

19 **Listen now to my voice; I will give you counsel, and God will be with you: Stand before God for the people, so that you may bring the difficulties to God.**

20 **And you shall teach them the statutes and the laws, and show them the way in which they must walk and the work they must do.**

21 **Moreover you shall select from all the people able men, such as fear God, men of truth, hating covetousness; and place such over them to be rulers of thousands, rulers of hundreds, rulers of fifties, and rulers of tens.**

22 **And LET THEM judge the people at all times. Then it will be that every great matter they shall bring to you, but every small matter they themselves shall judge. So it will be easier for you, for they will bear the burden with you.**

23 **If you do this thing, and God so commands you, then you will be able to endure, and all this people will also go to their place in peace."**

Perhaps two of the most difficult words for Moses to hear were *"let them"* (v. 22). Perfectionists have a hard time letting other people do the work. Perhaps subconsciously, perfectionists often believe that no one else can do the job as well as they can. They think they have to do everything if they want it done correctly. Such thinking can produce positive results on a short-term basis, but ultimately this way of working has its limitations and can even be quite destructive.

Even though Moses learned about delegation through Jethro's counsel, he was still struggling several months later with the tendency to do everything on his own. The pressure of bearing this overwhelming burden led him to tell the Lord, *"I am not able to bear all these people alone, because the burden is too heavy for me. If You treat me like this, please kill me here and now—if I have found favor in Your sight—and do not let me see my wretchedness!"* (Num. 11:14-15). God responded to Moses' distress in a compassionate and generous way. Instead of simply appointing other people to help him, God told Moses, *"...I will take of the Spirit that is upon you and will put the same upon them; and they shall bear the burden of the people with you, that you may not bear it yourself alone"* (Num. 11:17-18).

It is important to note that this impartation of the Spirit was not so that other people would take over Moses' place of leadership. This impartation was meant to equip and enable other people *to help* Moses in the carrying out of his leadership responsibilities (see Numbers 11:10-17,24-30).

Moses Had a Timothy

According to Exodus 24:13, Joshua was Moses' assistant. Joshua was to Moses in the Old Testament what Timothy was to Paul in the New Testament. Joshua followed Moses faithfully and served him diligently. Joshua also embraced the mission God had given Moses.

Joshua's commitment to Moses transcended commitment to a man; Joshua was also deeply committed to God. Exodus chapter 33 says, "As Moses went into the tent, the pillar of cloud would come down and stay at the entrance, while the

Lord spoke with Moses. The Lord would speak to Moses face to face, as a man speaks with his friend. Then Moses would return to the camp, but his young assistant Joshua son of Nun did not leave the tent" (vv. 9–11 *NIV*). We would do well to follow Joshua's example. Yes, we serve the leader, but we also maintain a strong relationship with God Himself.

The Building of the Tabernacle

We are studying how the help of other people greatly contributed to Moses' ministry. We've seen that Aaron and Joshua were his foremost helpers, but Moses enlisted the aid of others to help him carry out his divine assignment.

When the time came to establish the priesthood and to build the tabernacle, God gave Moses a specific plan and said, *"See to it that you make them according to the pattern which was shown you on the mountain"* (Exod. 25:40). God showed Moses the building blueprint, so to speak, but Moses didn't do any of the actual building. Moses was instructed to utilize gifted workers to whom God had given wisdom, knowledge, and understanding (Exod. 28:3; 31:2–6). Exodus 39:42–43 says, "So the people of Israel followed all of the Lord's instructions to Moses. Moses inspected all their work and blessed them because it had been done as the Lord had commanded him" (*NLT*).

The tabernacle was blessed for several reasons:
1. When instructing the workers, Moses followed the pattern God gave him.
2. Even though he was the one with the plan, Moses didn't try to do the work himself. He trusted others to follow the plan.
3. Moses enlisted talented, skilled people who had the wisdom of God for the given tasks.
4. The people to whom the tasks were assigned followed Moses' instructions instead of trying to do things their own way.

Each of these four principles are important for *today's* leaders and followers to remember. The tabernacle was a success for several reasons, and when we follow these same biblical principles, we can be successful as well.

In terms of modern leadership principles, Moses might be considered a micromanager in light of these passages, but keep in mind that the tabernacle had major prophetic significance. Hebrews 8:5 says that it was *"the copy and shadow of the heavenly things."* Hence, anything that deviated from the pattern God had shown Moses would send a false prophetic message about Christ and His redemptive work.

While leaders today typically do not (and should not) try to micromanage *every detail* of what their key leaders do, some oversight is natural and good. There are core values and priorities that the pastor desires to see reflected in every department and ministry of the church. Staff members and supportive ministers should make sure their work within the church reflects the pastor's core values and priorities.

Moses was a great man of God, but he could have never accomplished what he did without the assistance of helpers—those people who not only accepted responsibilities and carried out tasks, but who also were anointed by and walked in the same Spirit.

QUESTIONS FOR REFLECTION AND DISCUSSION

1. Aaron and Hur held up the hands of Moses as Joshua led the military against the Amalekites. Do you see this happening in your church? Who is holding up the hands of the pastor? Who is holding up the hands of the pastoral staff?

2. In Numbers chapter 11 we read that the Spirit that was upon Moses also came upon his helpers. Do you believe that the same Spirit anointed your pastor has also anointed you? Do you sense the Holy Spirit equipping and enabling you to assist in carrying out the purpose of God in your church?

3. Joshua was very loyal and faithful to Moses, but his commitment to God transcended his relationship to Moses. Do you only relate to God in terms of your relationship to your pastor and your work in the church? Or does your relationship with God go beyond your natural relationships and duties?
4. In order for the tabernacle to be built and the garments of the high priest to be made, it was necessary that the assigned workers be gifted in highly technical areas and that they still do their work according to the pattern that God showed Moses. How does this apply in your church?
5. What did you learn from this chapter and how can you apply it?
6. What areas do you need to pray about or improve in?

CHAPTER 12

David and Jonathan: Knitted Souls

The soul of Jonathan was knit to the soul of David, and Jonathan loved him as his own soul...

Then Jonathan and David made a covenant, because he loved him as his own soul.

And Jonathan took off the robe that was on him and gave it to David, with his armor, even to his sword and his bow and his belt.

−1 Samuel 18:1,3−4

And David was in the Wilderness of Ziph in a forest.

Then Jonathan, Saul's son, arose and went to David in the woods and strengthened his hand in God.

And he said to him, "Do not fear, for the hand of Saul my father shall not find you. You shall be king over Israel, and I shall be next to you. Even my father Saul knows that."

−1 Samuel 23:15−17

The Bible makes it clear that God called David and raised him up to be king of Israel. Naturally speaking, however, if it had not been for Jonathan, there might never have been a

King David. God used Jonathan, the son of King Saul, to protect David, which enabled David to eventually ascend to the throne. Even though Jonathan was the rightful heir, he refused to participate in his father's jealousy and even put his own life on the line for David (see 1 Samuel 19:1–2; 20:30–33).

When Jonathan died, David said, *"I am distressed for you, my brother Jonathan; You have been very pleasant to me; Your love to me was wonderful, Surpassing the love of women"* (2 Sam. 1:26). Jonathan's death greatly affected David, who more than recognized the tremendous contribution Jonathan had made to his life.

'Whatever You Decide'

'DO WHAT YOU THINK IS BEST. I'M WITH YOU COMPLETELY, WHATEVER YOU DECIDE.'

You may have heard teaching on the devotion and loyalty of Jonathan's armor-bearer. Where do you think the armor-bearer picked up those traits? Jonathan himself demonstrated that uncommon kind of devotion and loyalty toward David. These attributes were part of Jonathan's character and not just a one-time event.

What kind of devotion and loyalty did Jonathan's armor-bearer display? A kind that yielded to their leader's decision—no matter what their leader decided.

1 SAMUEL 14:6–7 (*NLT*)

6 **"Let's go across to see those pagans," Jonathan said to his armor bearer. "Perhaps the Lord will help us, for nothing can hinder the Lord. He can win a battle whether he has many warriors or only a few!"**

7 **"Do what you think is best," the youth replied. "I'm with you completely, whatever you decide."**

Countless pastors around the world would love to hear that statement coming from those around them. *Do what you think is best, Pastor. We're with you completely, whatever you decide.*

As supportive ministers, our efforts cannot be geared toward self-advancement. Our efforts must be geared toward making *others* successful. That's the attitude that Timothy had toward Paul. That's the attitude that John the Baptist had toward Jesus. That's the attitude Joshua had toward Moses. And that's the attitude we see in Jonathan's relationship with David.

I don't want you to misunderstand me; Jonathan didn't put David on a pedestal and worship him. But Jonathan recognized God's hand and call upon David's life. Jonathan didn't exalt a personality; he furthered a purpose.

In spiritually profitable ministry, there ought to be divine connections where relationships are not merely functional or professional, but where there is a supernatural knitting together of hearts. When we join our hearts, abilities, and efforts together, God's Kingdom will be greatly advanced in the earth.

QUESTIONS FOR REFLECTION AND DISCUSSION

1. What does it mean to you when you read, "The soul of Jonathan was knit to the soul of David"?
2. What caused Jonathan to promote and protect David when he could have promoted himself?
3. Do what you think is best, Pastor. I'm with you completely, whatever you decide. Does that phrase reflect your attitude?
4. Have you ever had a tendency to drag your feet when asked to do something instead of the supportive attitude expressed by Jonathon's armor bearer?
5. What did you learn from this chapter and how can you apply it?
6. What areas do you need to pray about or improve in?

David and His Brave Warriors

Other Benjamites and some men from Judah also came to David in his stronghold.

David went out to meet them and said to them, "If you have come to me in peace, to help me, I am ready to have you unite with me. But if you have come to betray me to my enemies when my hands are free from violence, may the God of our fathers see it and judge you."

—1 Chronicles 12:16–17 (*NIV*)

David wanted whoever helped him to possess certain character traits. One thing David required of his "mighty men" (his leadership team) was that they "come in peace" (v. 17). David surrounded himself with people who sought to help him not hurt him—people who wanted to support the vision God had put in his heart, not to hinder it.

Just like David, pastors today are looking for people who will come to them in peace. While pastors appreciate people coming to them with talent, that's not a pastor's first consideration in considering potential team members. Attitude and motives (*"If you have come to me in peace…"*) are foremost in a leader's thinking. People with a critical nature—those who constantly create dissension and strife—cause more damage to a team than any benefit they might bring with their talents.

Have You Come to Help?

In the passage we read in First Chronicles chapter 12, David not only wanted to know if the men were coming in peace, but he also wanted to know if they had come to help him. He knew that the job ahead required more than passive spectators; David needed people who would be active participants—people eager and willing to work.

I've heard statistics that indicate a staggering trend concerning churches in America today. It is estimated that *80 percent* of the people in our churches have no ministry in their local church! In other words, only 20 percent of the congregation volunteers, serves, or works in any capacity. How would your physical body function if 80 percent of it were paralyzed and non-functioning? David needed people who had a heart to help, and pastors today need the same!

Under Nehemiah's leadership, the wall of Jerusalem was rebuilt with amazing speed because, *"the people had a mind to work"* (Neh. 4:6). Believers today must be on guard against becoming become lazy. It's true that we are not saved *by* works, but it is also true that we are saved *unto* works (see Ephesians 2:8). In other words, works are not the *cause* of our salvation, but they are to be a *result* of our salvation. Works are not the *root* of our salvation, but they are to be the *fruit* of our salvation.

United Hearts

David told a group of volunteers, "If you've come to me in peace and have come to help me, 'I am ready to have you unite with me'" (1 Chron. 12:17 *NIV*). The *New King James Version* says, *"My heart will be united with you."* Pastors don't want their volunteers or staff members to merely perform a task; pastors want to sense a spiritual union with their supportive ministers as they carry out the purpose and mission of the church. Leaders recognize the need for a knitting together of hearts—that divine connection—in order to fulfill the will of God together.

The Work of the Spirit Produces Loyalty

In First Chronicles 12:16–17, we've seen David's "investigation" of the people who wanted to serve with him. What happened next in this passage is truly remarkable.

1 CHRONICLES 12:18 (*NIV*)
18 Then the Spirit came upon Amasai, chief of the Thirty, and he said: "We are yours, O David! We are with you, O son of Jesse! Success, success to you, and success to those who help you, for your God will help you." So David received them and made them leaders of his raiding bands.

This verse says the Holy Spirit came upon Amasai, a respected leader, causing Amasai to utter words that must have blessed David to hear: "We are yours, O David! We are with you, O son of Jesse! Success, success to you, and success to those who help you, for your God will help you."

There are many manifestations that can occur when the Holy Spirit moves upon a person, but perhaps none are as welcome to a visionary leader as the fruit of loyalty that came forth from Amasai. These thirty men were committed to the success of David on a personal level, and they believed in the purpose and the mission to which David was called. They pledged themselves to the success of David and to the assignment God had given him.

That word "success" which Amasai spoke toward David in verse 18 is the Hebrew word "shalom." It refers to *completeness, wholeness, and soundness in every dimension of one's being: spiritually, emotionally, socially, physically, and financially.* Pastors want and need people around them who are committed to the success of the vision God has put in their hearts. It becomes a mutual commitment, because true spiritual leaders and pastors are also committed to the success of those who help them.

Haggai 1:3–11 explains that when God's people see to it that *His* house is blessed God will see to it that *their* houses are blessed as well. Natural leaders can and should put this spiritual principle into practice when it comes to caring for the very people who so loyally care for them.

Warriors and Commanders

> IT'S NECESSARY TO HAVE SOME COMMANDERS, BUT IT CREATES MAJOR PROBLEMS IF EVERYONE IN THE CHURCH WANTS TO BE A COMMANDER.

Our key text for this chapter is found in First Chronicles chapter 12. *First*, we learned that some Benjamites and some men from Judah came to David to join his band of soldiers. *Second*, we read that they came in peace. *Third*, these men came in order to help David. *Fourth*, their hearts were united to David, and they were committed to his success.

Let's continue reading with verse 21 and see how these men began to function in two similar yet different categories—*brave warriors* and *commanders*.

1 CHRONICLES 12:21 (*NIV*)

21 They helped David against raiding bands, for all of them were brave warriors, and they were commanders in his army.

While both categories of men were active in David's army and may have shared some of the same tasks, each also had a different role with differing responsibilities. *Warriors* are the front-line, down-in-the-trenches, roll-up-the-sleeves-and-get-the-work-done type. These people are tremendously valuable in the church; nothing would get done without them. *Commanders* are leaders. It's necessary to have some commanders, but it creates major problems if everyone in the church wants to be a commander. Churches need both warriors and commanders.

This passage in First Chronicles chapter 12 closes with this powerful statement: "Day after day men came to help David, until he had a great army, like the army of God" (v. 22 *NIV*). May this same statement be made regarding Christian workers and supportive ministers. May pastors and leaders throughout the world experience a daily inflow of men and women who come to them in peace, willing to help, and ready to unite their heart in common purpose.

David's Mighty Men

So far in this chapter, we've gleaned several leadership and follower-ship principles from the story regarding Amasai and the build-up of David's army. Now I want to look at the principles revealed in a story about three of David's "mighty men" as told in First Chronicles chapter 11. This particular story about these men gives us rich insight into what caused the deep, mutual sense of loyalty and devotion between David and his followers.

1 CHRONICLES 11:15–19

15 Now three of the thirty chief men went down to the rock to David, into the cave of Adullam; and the army of the Philistines encamped in the Valley of Rephaim.

16 David was then in the stronghold, and the garrison of the Philistines was then in Bethlehem.

17 And David said with longing, "Oh, that someone would give me a drink of water from the well of Bethlehem, which is by the gate!"

18 So the three broke through the camp of the Philistines, drew water from the well of Bethlehem that was by the gate, and took it and brought it to David. Nevertheless David would not drink it, but poured it out to the Lord.

19 And he said, "Far be it from me, O my God, that I should do this! Shall I drink the blood of these men who have put their lives in jeopardy? For at the risk of their lives

they brought it." Therefore he would not drink it. These things were done by the three mighty men.

The commitment and dedication of these three men is obvious. Even though it wasn't David's intention for them to do so, they risked their lives to honor their leader's sentimental wish for water from a certain well in his hometown.

When these men brought the water to David he refused to drink it, pouring it out unto the Lord instead. In our modern thinking, we might consider David's action one of grave disrespect. However, in the mind of these three warriors, David's action was the highest expression of honor and respect he could have possibly shown them.

"Drink offerings" poured out to God were a form of Old Testament worship, and through his actions David was, in effect, saying to these men: "Your act of devotion is too sacred for me to flippantly consume in a self-indulgent way. Your dedication is too holy for me to use on gratifying my flesh. The only appropriate course of action is for me to take your sacrificial gift and offer it to God Himself in worship. This demonstrates the truth that you are ultimately serving God, not me."

When David's followers saw his display of worship unto the Lord, it no doubt strengthened their commitment and their loyalty to David. They saw that he was not exploiting or taking advantage of their service in a self-serving way. It communicated to them that David saw the big picture–that their service wasn't really about *David* and the preeminence of *his* personal desires, but about *God's* purposes and the fulfillment of *His* plans.

Have you come in peace to your church? Are you eager and willing to help your pastor? I trust that your heart will be united and knit together with the heart of your pastor as you commit to the common cause of faithfully fulfilling God's purposes and plans.

QUESTIONS FOR REFLECTION AND DISCUSSION

1. Is your church full of people who have come in peace and who have come to help? Name some of them.

2. Are you excited about the success of your pastor and of the vision that God has given for your church? If you are, how do you express your excitement? If you aren't, what do you need to do to become motivated?

3. Are you as committed to the success of God's House as you are to your own house?

4. Do you have a good balance in your church between commanders and warriors?

5. What stood out to you about the dedication of the three men who risked their lives for David in First Chronicles 11:15–19?

6. What stood out to you concerning the honor that David showed to his men by offering their sacrificial gift to the Lord?

7. What did you learn from this chapter and how can you apply it?

8. What areas do you need to pray about or improve in?

Elisha: An Example of True Follower-ship

I n the first half of his ministry, Elijah was a "do-it-yourself" type of minister. Though he was used powerfully by God, there was no sense of partnership or teamwork operating in Elijah's life or ministry. It was from this sense of isolation that he said three times, "I am the only one left" (1 Kings 18:22; 19:10,14 *NIV*). Part of God's answer to Elijah's "alone-ness" was to direct him to anoint Elisha—a young man who would eventually succeed Elijah as prophet (1 Kings 19:16). Before he became prophet, Elisha first became Elijah's servant and assistant for many years.

By studying the story of Elijah and Elisha we can learn several principles regarding leadership and follower-ship. First, let's look at the level of resolve Elisha had when it came to whole-heartedly following Elijah.

Elisha was plowing the fields when the prophet Elijah came and threw his cloak over him, symbolic of the prophetic call and the anointing of the Holy Spirit. First Kings 19:21 says, "Elisha then returned to his oxen, killed them, and used the wood from the plow to build a fire to roast their flesh. He passed around the meat to the other plowmen, and they all ate. Then he went with Elijah as his assistant" (*NLT*).

What can we learn from this verse of scripture? First, we see that Elisha took it very seriously when Elijah (and God) called him into ministry. Second, Elisha didn't waste any time in following his leader. He didn't dilly-dally and debate whether he should or shouldn't heed the call of God on his life. Third, once he made his decision, Elisha didn't look back or preserve anything of his former life to fall back on "just in case." No, he "put his hand to the plow" in the figurative sense that the Bible talks of in Luke 9:61–62 and never looked back. This kind of resolve in following Elijah (and ultimately the plan of God for his life) sets an example for today's supportive ministers.

> ONCE ELISHA BEGAN TO SERVE AND ASSIST ELIJAH, ELIJAH NEVER AGAIN COMPLAINED TO GOD, "I AM LEFT ALONE."

Faithful to Follow

The kind of resolve Elisha demonstrated in the beginning of serving Elijah is the same kind of resolve he exhibited at the end of his service—and throughout his own ministry. Elisha was a steady, determined minister who served with heartfelt commitment and zeal.

In Second Kings chapter 2, we find Elijah nearing the day when he was taken up to heaven. As Elijah continued to travel and minister, he repeatedly tried to leave Elisha behind. Before moving from one town to another, Elijah told Elisha, "Stay here." Again and again, Elisha responded, *"...As the Lord lives, and as your soul lives, I will not leave you!"* (2 Kings 2:2,4,6). The rest of the "sons of the prophets" were content to observe Elijah from a distance, but Elisha was determined to accompany Elijah to the very end.

Once Elisha began to serve and assist Elijah, Elijah never again complained to God, "I am left alone." Can your pastor truly say he has the help he needs? Or, has the type of assistance or attitude rendered to him in the past caused him to feel "left alone" in the ministry?

When Elijah was no longer on the scene and King Jehoshaphat was in need of guidance, he asked, *"Is there no prophet of the Lord here, that we may inquire of the Lord by him?"* The answer he received was, *"Elisha the son of Shaphat is here, who poured water on the hands of Elijah"* (2 Kings 3:11). Elisha was not noted here for his great teaching or preaching skills, but as one who served and assisted Elijah. Elisha's reputation in serving Elijah is what brought him before the king where he could then minister and carry on the great work to which God had called him through Elijah.

As supportive ministers seeking to walk in the steps of Timothy and the other godly examples we have studied so far, we should emulate Elisha's behavior in the kind of dedicated service he offered Elijah. Elisha didn't seek to promote his own ministry, but only tried to promote and serve Elijah. He also refused to turn back to his former walk of life or to resign himself to watching Elijah from the sidelines. He followed Elijah every step of the way—in spirit and in action, and when Elijah finally went to be with the Lord, Elisha stepped into the next dimension of ministry that God prescribed for him.

QUESTIONS FOR REFLECTION AND DISCUSSION

1. When Elisha was called to be Elijah's assistant and to eventually succeed him in his prophetic office, he killed the oxen he had plowed with, used the wood from the plow to build a fire, and held a feast for the people. What does this say about Elisha's commitment to his new assignment?
2. What impact did Elisha have on Elijah's life and ministry?
3. In terms of their callings and in their relationship to Elijah, what differentiated Elisha from the rest of the sons of the prophets?

4. Do you try to be known for your talents and/or preaching skills? Or do you strive to be known for your faithful service and follower-ship?
5. What did you learn from this chapter and how can you apply it?
6. What areas do you need to pray about or improve in?

PART III

The Traits of Great Supportive Ministers

I n the first two parts of this book, we've outlined biblical principles and examples of supportive ministry. In this next section, we will study a number of positive character traits that every supportive minister ought to possess. These traits will make you an invaluable asset to any leader in any field–especially to pastors in ministry.

If any of these traits are not currently present in your character, begin to develop and create those traits. If the traits are present, but lacking in some way, continue to strengthen them. And if you find that you already possess some of these traits to the fullest extent possible, I encourage you to strive to build upon those traits until you fully possess them all.

Great Supportive Ministers Are Loyal

And he commanded them, saying, "Thus you shall act in the fear of the Lord, faithfully and with a loyal heart."

−2 Chronicles 19:9

Loyalty is an internal devotion, a commitment to a relationship and to the welfare of another. *Merriam-Webster's Collegiate Dictionary, Tenth Edition,* defines the word "loyal" as *unswerving in allegiance; faithful to a person to whom fidelity is due;* and *faithful to a cause or ideal.* Some people develop an appearance of loyalty, but inwardly they harbor ill will and rebellion. Loyalty is deeper than outward compliance. It implies being faithful and true, not treacherous or undermining.

The Bible is full of men and women who demonstrated the kind of loyalty we ought to have as supportive ministers. In this chapter, we will take a look at just a few.

Ruth exhibited strong loyalty when she said to Naomi, "Don't urge me to leave you or to turn back from you. Where you go I will go, and where you stay I will stay. Your people will be my people and your God my God. Where you die I will die, and there I will be buried..." (Ruth 1:16–17 *NIV*).

In Second Samuel chapter 15 we find the contrast of a disloyal and rebellious son and a loyal and submissive servant. Though distressed by the rebellion of Absalom, King David must have been encouraged and refreshed by the loyalty he discovered in Ittai the Gittite. As David was preparing to evacuate Jerusalem and flee from the insurgency that Absalom had started, he had the following encounter:

2 SAMUEL 15:19–21 (*NIV*)

19 The king said to Ittai the Gittite, "Why should you come along with us? Go back and stay with King Absalom. You are a foreigner, an exile from your homeland.

20 You came only yesterday. And today shall I make you wander about with us, when I do not know where I am going? Go back, and take your countrymen. May kindness and faithfulness be with you."

21 But Ittai replied to the king, "As surely as the Lord lives, and as my lord the king lives, wherever my lord the king may be, whether it means life or death, there will your servant be."

> SOME PEOPLE DEVELOP AN APPEARANCE OF LOYALTY, BUT INWARDLY THEY HARBOR ILL WILL AND REBELLION.

Ittai was loyal in his heart and actions to his king. Even when the king's own son turned against him, Ittai was loyal. This kind of loyalty is rare these days, but it ought to be the aim of every supportive minister.

King David also found great loyalty in his military leaders. Second Samuel 12:26–28 says, *"Now Joab fought against Rabbah of the people of Ammon, and took the royal city. And Joab sent messengers to David, and said, 'I have fought against Rabbah, and I have taken the city's water supply. Now therefore, gather the rest of the people together and encamp against the city and take it, lest I take the city and it be called after my name.'"* This passage reveals that Joab didn't want to receive credit for his own accomplishments. He wasn't out to make a name for himself or to draw attention and accolades. He wanted to bring honor to his leader and preferred the captured city be named after David instead of himself (v. 28).

Ruth, Ittai, and Joab offer us examples of what it means to be loyal. Ruth was loyal to her mother-in-law; Ittai was loyal to his king; and Joab was loyal to his commander-in-chief. Supportive ministers can apply this same principle of loyalty to their pastor and other leaders.

Defend and Protect Your Pastor

Many years ago I went to see an elderly lady in the hospital; when I sat down beside her bed she patted me on the hand and said, "Brother Cooke, I want to thank you for coming to see me. The senior pastor hasn't been by to see me." There was something in her tone of voice that immediately told me she was offended that the senior pastor had not come to see her. There was a critical and cutting attitude behind her reference to him.

I could have capitalized on her being disgruntled toward the pastor and used the opportunity to promote myself. I could have said, "Well, ma'am, I'm here because I have such a love for the people." *But it's never right for a staff member to make himself look good at the pastor's expense.* (It may be helpful for supportive ministers to remember that the only reason they have a position in the church is because of the pastor!)

One of our jobs as a supportive minister is to represent our pastor and other team members in a favorable light, especially when others make unfair criticisms. In this situation where the lady I was visiting made negative comments about the senior pastor, I responded by saying something to this effect: "I am glad to be here to visit you, but the reason I'm here is because the senior pastor asked me to come. God has given our pastor the wisdom to know that he can't be everywhere at once, and that's why he hired people like me to be part of his staff. Just this morning he asked me to stop by and check on you, because he wants to know how you're doing. I'm here on his behalf, because he cares about you."

(It's really not a compliment to you if someone feels like he can insult the pastor in your presence and get you to side with him. He's basically saying that he thinks he can buy you with his words. He sees a price tag on you and thinks you can be bought with flattery. It's not a compliment when people think that about you. Strong supportive ministers have a reputation of honor, and people know those supportive ministers will never take sides against their pastor.)

Does Loyalty Equal Blind Obedience?

You may wonder if I'm advising you to blindly comply with anything and everything your pastor says and does. Let me ask you to define the source of your disagreements: Is your pastor walking according to God's Word—or in blatant disregard of the Bible? In other words, are your disagreements with your pastor over procedural things (ideas, methods, vision, and so forth), or are they related to moral and ethical issues? I like what Dan Reiland said about loyalty in his book *Shoulder to Shoulder*:

> Loyalty to the pastor does not mean blindly following and agreeing with everything he says or does. It means that as long as the pastor is giving biblical leadership, as a leader, you are to support your pastor even if you might do things differently yourself.[1]

In other words, as long as your pastor isn't doing something immoral, illegal, or unethical, learn to go with the flow—even if you would do things a different way.

Reiland went on to provide the following commentary as advice to those who wonder how to respond to criticisms against their pastor:

As a leader you must speak up with a positive focus in support of your pastor. Put him in a good light. You might be thinking, *What if I don't agree with the pastor but do with the one complaining?* You may disagree with your pastor–some of your greatest value will come from your honesty with him. Expressing those thoughts, however, must be done in private between you and your pastor. A leader forfeits his right to do or say anything that will hurt the church. Undermining the pastor's leadership will definitely hurt the church. God blesses unity, not division. Express your thoughts and feelings with your pastor freely in private, but in public, support him 100 percent.[2]

Promote the Pastor

As a church leader, there may be times when people will present an idea to you and ask you to share it with the pastor. You could go back to them later and say, "I thought your idea was great, but the pastor said no." That kind of response does not promote goodwill toward the pastor.

Remember, your job as a staff member is not to promote your own popularity, to build your own kingdom within the church, or to make yourself look good by making someone else look bad. Your job is to promote the pastor, to build his vision within the church, and to encourage people to follow his leadership.

So how *should* you respond to people when the pastor doesn't embrace what someone considered to be a good idea? Wanting to honor the pastor and realizing that people can be offended when their ideas are not accepted, it would be better to give this type of response: "I don't think we're going to be acting on your idea at this time, but thanks so much for your interest in the church. Please don't hesitate to share other ideas in the future."

This type of reply allows you to tell the truth and to respond to their idea–but to do so without promoting your own popularity and without making the pastor look like the bad guy who shot down their idea.

Loyalty Is the Anchor That Steadies You

Being a loyal person doesn't mean that you always agree with the pastor or that you never experience frustration in your work for the church. We will face disagreements and frustrations in every line of work and in every relationship. But loyalty provides stability in those situations. Loyalty is the anchor that steadies you in tough times.

For example, in a marriage you will face occasional challenges, but having already committed in your heart to be loyal to your spouse provides an anchor that will steady you in the difficult seasons. Thankfully, you won't have to figure out if you are going to stay in the relationship or leave the marriage, because you have already settled that issue in your heart. Therefore, loyalty allows you to focus all your attention and energies on resolving the conflict.

In a church or ministry relationship, you may become frustrated with someone or something, but if you're following in Timothy's footsteps and becoming the supportive minister God wants you to be, then you've already chosen to be mature and to walk in love. You may still discuss issues and still not see eye-to-eye on everything, but you realize that the overall purpose is more important than the matter about which you disagree.

Loyalty Makes for Positive Transitions

As a key leader or worker in a church, loyalty doesn't necessarily mean you'll be at that church your entire life, but it does mean that while you are under the umbrella of that pastor's leadership, you will give him the very best you have to give. During your time there, you will always seek and promote the welfare of that church—dedicated to being an asset, not a liability.

If a transition does occur, loyalty means that you'll transition in a positive way. You won't plant negative seeds as you leave or talk badly about the church once you're gone. You will never conduct yourself in a way that undermines your former church or its leadership. Loyalty demands that you always walk in honor, courtesy, and respect.

We must diligently seek each other's welfare if we are to be successful in God's eyes. Loyalty is a vital expression of the love of God, and it is a key ingredient in ministry relationships and ministry success.

QUESTIONS FOR REFLECTION AND DISCUSSION

1. What do you think of the following statement? Some people develop an appearance of being loyal, but inwardly they are harboring ill will and rebellion.
2. It seems that loyalty is not as high a value in people's lives today as it used to be. Why do you think that is?
3. What does "representing the pastor and other team members favorably" mean to you?
4. What did you learn from this chapter and how can you apply it?
5. What areas do you need to pray about or improve in?

---

[1] Dan Reiland, *Shoulder to Shoulder* (Nashville: Thomas Nelson Publishers, 1997), 170.

[2] Dan Reiland, *Shoulder to Shoulder* (Nashville: Thomas Nelson Publishers, 1997), 170–171.

Great Supportive Ministers Have Excellent Attitudes

For the Kingdom of God is not a matter of what we eat or drink, but of living a life of goodness and peace and joy in the Holy Spirit.

If you serve Christ with this attitude, you will please God. And other people will approve of you, too.

So then, let us aim for harmony in the church and try to build each other up.

—Romans 14:17–19 (*NLT*)

The importance of attitude cannot be overestimated; it is one of the top factors that determine the quality of a supportive minister's contribution to the local church. You could approach any pastor with two potential leaders/workers: Candidate A has phenomenal talent but a poor attitude, while Candidate B has decent talent but a great attitude. Most pastors will not hesitate to choose Candidate B because they know that no matter how talented a person is, he will ultimately create problems on the team if he has a bad attitude.

GOOD ATTITUDES ARE CONTAGIOUS; THEY INSPIRE AND ENCOURAGE OTHERS.

As an associate pastor, I saw that the senior pastor had to deal with many different responsibilities and problems on a continual basis. I made up my mind that I would not add to his list of responsibilities and problems. I endeavored to lift him up, not drag him down. I wanted to make his job easier, not harder. Every supportive minister should endeavor to be a low-maintenance, high-output team member.

Having the right attitude not only makes a supportive minister a blessing to the senior pastor, but it can also help to motivate the rest of the team members. Good attitudes are contagious; they inspire and encourage others. Bad attitudes are also contagious; they can create a negative and hostile work environment and make others feel uncomfortable—like they have to walk on eggshells all the time.

People who have bad attitudes often blame their disposition on others or on various circumstances, but the fact is that each of us is responsible for our own attitude. Viktor E. Frankl, survivor of a Nazi concentration camp, said, "Everything can be taken from a man but one thing: the last of the human freedoms—to choose one's attitude in any given set of circumstances, to choose one's own way."[1] You are free to choose your attitude—make a good choice.

How Important Is Attitude?

Your perspective, or the way you look at things, greatly influences the type of attitude you have. One person said, "Two men looked through prison bars; one saw mud, the other saw stars." In any situation, you can choose what you are going to focus and dwell on. There will always be flaws, shortcomings, and imperfections in any relationship or organization, and if you choose to focus on these things, you will remain agitated and frustrated. Instead, you can choose to focus on the good things that are taking place, which will boost your spirits and your attitude.

How important is attitude? Its significance is huge–practically inestimable! You may have great talent, but without a great attitude to go along with it your ultimate contribution can be totally undermined. You may have a great call and a great anointing upon your life, but without a great attitude your effectiveness will be greatly diminished. You may have tremendous experience and a great education, but you're still not going to be productive in the long run without a great attitude. And the most amazing thing about attitude is that it really boils down to a simple choice– a choice to be positive encouraging, pleasant, cooperative, and supportive.

How much will having the right attitude help you? How much will having the wrong attitude hold you back? As one individual said, "Nothing can stop the man with the right mental attitude from achieving his goal; nothing on earth can help the man with the wrong mental attitude."[2]

QUESTIONS FOR REFLECTION AND DISCUSSION

1. Do you maintain a good attitude in your work?
2. What do you do to stay positive when you encounter negative circumstances or difficult people?
3. Are you a pleasant, positive person to be around?
4. Does your attitude lift and encourage your pastor? Your coworkers?
5. If someone around you has a bad attitude, do you let it drag you down?
6. How do you maintain a good attitude when those around you have a bad attitude?
7. What did you learn from this chapter and how can you apply it?
8. What areas do you need to pray about or improve in?

[1] Viktor E. Frankl, *Man's Search for Meaning* (Boston: Beacon Press, 1992), 75.

[2] W.W. Ziege, quoted in Ted Goodman, ed., *The Forbes Book of Business Quotations* (New York: Black Dog & Leventhal Publishers, 1997), 80.

Great Supportive Ministers Are Faithful

*His lord said to him, "Well done, good and FAITHFUL
SERVANT; YOU WERE FAITHFUL OVER A FEW THINGS, I
will make you ruler over many things. Enter into the joy of
your lord."*

—Matthew 25:21

We know from this passage in Matthew and from other
scriptures that God places high value on faithfulness. We
know how important faithfulness is to the marriage relationship,
but what about the working relationship? I believe every boss,
pastor, and leader in the world would rejoice if every one of their
employees and volunteer workers possessed great faithfulness.

We've learned that supportive ministers are supposed to be
faithful, but what exactly does that mean in the context of
working in church or ministry? The following is a list of some
of the characteristics of faithfulness; see how many of these
traits are present in your work ethic:

Traits of Faithful People

• Careful to fulfill a promise; reliable; you can believe them
• Dedicated in carrying out duties and responsibilities

- Diligent in work
- Dependable in completing assignments; you can count on their work being done
- Thorough; not just a good starter, but also a great finisher; doesn't "drop the ball" halfway through the project
- Pays attention to details; doesn't let things "fall through the cracks"
- Punctual; shows up on time and meets deadlines
- Consistent and constant; not up one day and down the next
- Doesn't just look good on the surface, but is solid through and through
- Honest and trustworthy; isn't underhanded or sneaky
- Meets and exceeds expectations; doesn't do just enough to get by; is willing to go the extra mile

This list should give you a good idea of how faithfulness is demonstrated in an everyday work environment. Now to give you an idea of the kind of results faithfulness will produce, let's read a passage from Genesis chapter 39.

GENESIS 39:2–6 (*NLT*)

2   The Lord was with Joseph and blessed him greatly as he served in the home of his Egyptian master.

3   Potiphar noticed this and realized that the Lord was with Joseph, giving him success in everything he did.

4   So Joseph naturally became quite a favorite with him. Potiphar soon put Joseph in charge of his entire household and entrusted him with all his business dealings.

5   From the day Joseph was put in charge, the Lord began to bless Potiphar for Joseph's sake. All his household affairs began to run smoothly, and his crops and livestock flourished.

6   So Potiphar gave Joseph complete administrative responsibility over everything he owned. With Joseph there, he didn't have a worry in the world, except to decide what he wanted to eat!

Joseph is an outstanding biblical example of a faithful person. Even when he was sold as a slave in Egypt, his diligence and reliability remained steadfast. What were the results Joseph's faithfulness? He was trusted to rule over his employer's entire house and business and was given complete administrative responsibility over everything his boss owned (v. 6). Joseph's *faithfulness to the Lord* caused the Lord to bless Potiphar for Joseph's sake, and Joseph's *faithfulness to Potiphar* had immediate, tangible results as well: all the household affairs began to run smoothly, and Potiphar's crops and livestock flourished (v. 5). With Joseph in charge, Potiphar didn't have a care in the world!

Later, Joseph ended up in prison because of a false accusation, but he continued to be dependable, responsible, and faithful—to the Lord and to his overseers.

GENESIS 39:21–23 (*NLT*)
21 But the Lord was with Joseph there, too, and he granted Joseph favor with the chief jailer.
22 Before long, the jailer put Joseph in charge of all the other prisoners and over everything that happened in the prison.
23 The chief jailer had no more worries after that, because Joseph took care of everything. The Lord was with him, making everything run smoothly and successfully.

Even in jail Joseph's faithfulness was clearly evident and openly rewarded. Joseph was put in charge of all the other prisoners and, in effect, ran the prison in which he was held captive! Because he let Joseph take care of everything, the chief jailer had no more problems or worries.

Like Joseph, a faithful supportive minister today relieves his pastor (or supervisor) of detail work and mental clutter. If, however, a supportive minister is not dependable, the pastor will be burdened by those matters and will not be free to focus on the issues that should receive his attention.

Proverbs 25:19 says, "Putting confidence in an unreliable person is like chewing with a toothache or walking on a broken foot" (*NLT*). Great supportive ministers don't want to be a toothache or broken foot to their pastor or supervisor. They don't want to cause him pain and discomfort or make it difficult for him to do what needs to be done.

Proverbs 20:6 tells us, *"Most men will proclaim each his own goodness, But who can find a faithful man?"* It's not the *talkers* who are valuable contributors to the church, but the *doers*–the people who really get the job done! We should endeavor to be reliable supportive ministers. As Josh Billings said many years ago, "Be like a postage stamp. Stick to one thing until you get there."[1]

Faithful People Are Responsible

People who get the job done are faithful, and they are also *responsible*. They take initiative on projects and are also willing to take the blame if they make a mistake. Too few organizations have responsible workers. Some work environments are more like the following scenario:

> This is a story about four people: Everybody, Somebody, Anybody and Nobody. There was an important job to be done, and Everybody was asked to do it. Everybody was sure Somebody would do it. Anybody could have done it, but Nobody did it. Somebody got angry about that because it was Everybody's job. Everybody thought Anybody could do it. Nobody realized Everybody wouldn't do it. In the end, Everybody blamed Somebody when actually Nobody asked Anybody.[2]

Are you being irresponsible by allowing tasks to go undone because "it's not your job" or because it's not "big" enough to warrant your time and effort?

Some people fail the faithfulness test because they don't value what in their mind is a small task. In other words, they think, *When God gives me a really important assignment, then I'll be diligent and faithful.* In contrast, Helen Keller said, "I long to accomplish a great and noble task, but it is my chief duty to accomplish small tasks as if they were great and noble."[3] Thomas Jefferson once said, "He does most in God's great world who does his best in his own little world." [4] Anything you are assigned to do is big in God's eyes—and so is your faithfulness or lack of faithfulness in getting the job done.

Furthermore, your level of faithfulness determines the value of your service to your pastor and church. As your faithfulness decreases, so does your value. But be faithful, dependable, and thorough, and watch God use you mightily!

QUESTIONS FOR REFLECTION AND DISCUSSION

1. Look over The Traits of Faithful People listed below and take an inventory of your performance. On each trait, rate yourself on a scale from 1–10 and see how you are doing in the area of faithfulness.

    - Careful to fulfill a promise; reliable; you can believe them
      Your score: _____
    - Dedicated in carrying out duties and responsibilities
      Your score: _____
    - Diligent in work
      Your score: _____
    - Dependable in completing assignments; you can count on their work being done
      Your score: _____
    - Thorough; not just a good starter, but also a great finisher; doesn't "drop the ball" halfway through the project
      Your score: _____
    - Pays attention to details; doesn't let things "fall through the cracks"
      Your score: _____

- Punctual; shows up on time and meets deadlines
  Your score: _____
- Consistent and constant; not up one day and down the next
  Your score: _____
- Doesn't just look good on the surface, but is solid through and through
  Your score: _____
- Honest and trustworthy; isn't underhanded or sneaky
  Your score: _____
- Meets and exceeds expectations; doesn't do just enough to get by; is willing to go the extra mile
  Your score: _____

2. If your supervisor was handed the same inventory to fill out on your behalf, would he give you the same scores you gave yourself?
3. Are you like Joseph? When assignments are given to you, does your supervisor know that you'll get the job done thoroughly and with excellence?
4. Do you see the value of what some might consider "small things"? Do you carry out "small" tasks the same way you would carry out a "big" assignment?
5. What did you learn from this chapter and how can you apply it?
6. What areas do you need to pray about or improve in?

---

[1] *Wikiquote*, s.v. "Josh Billings," http://en.wikiquote.org/wiki/Josh_Billings.

[2] Nigel Rees, comp., *Cassell's Humorous Quotations* (London: Cassell, 2001), 59.

[3] Mark Water, ed., *The New Encyclopedia of Christian Quotations* (Grand Rapids: Baker Books, 2000), 351–352.

[4] Mark Water, ed., *The New Encyclopedia of Christian Quotations* (Grand Rapids: Baker Books, 2000), 351.

Great Supportive Ministers 'Play Well With Others'

I n the first few grades of elementary school, there was a particular designation on our report cards that read, "Plays well
with others." In addition to recording our progress in reading,
writing, and arithmetic, the teachers made note of how well we
got along with the other kids.
While *academic* or *technical*
skills are certainly important,
perhaps no other skill will
affect your effectiveness in
ministry more than your
social skills—how well you
relate to other people.

> While *academic* or *technical* skills are certainly important, perhaps no other skill will affect your effectiveness in ministry more than your *social* skills...

As a supportive minister, there are three main people or
groups of people where it is vital that you "play well with others."
First, you must get along and work well with the pastor. *Second*,
you must relate well to other leaders and to your coworkers.
Third, you must have a good relationship with the members of
the church.

Submission:
Relating Well to the Pastor

First, you must relate well to those in authority over you. In your job position, you may answer directly to your pastor, or there may be an immediate supervisor to whom you report and answer directly. In either case, a key factor in your success is your ability to submit to those in authority.

Hebrews 13:17 tells *how* we are to relate to those in authority and even tells us *why*. This scripture also tells us that causing our leaders grief would be unprofitable for us.

HEBREWS 13:17

17 OBEY THOSE WHO RULE OVER YOU, AND BE SUBMISSIVE, FOR THEY WATCH OUT FOR YOUR SOULS, **as those who must give account. Let them do so with joy and not with grief, for that would be unprofitable for you.**

When supportive ministers have a cooperative attitude, they enable the leaders to do their job joyfully and not with sorrow (*NLT*).

Here is one example of an *un*cooperative attitude and the sorrow that a supportive minister with this kind of attitude can cause.

A pastor told me that he had just started a church, and because he had such a small number of people, he had asked someone he did not know well to lead worship for him. The worship leader did a good job the first Sunday. Over the next few Sundays, the quality of the worship remained good, but the pastor noticed that the length of the praise and worship part of the service was getting progressively longer—to the point that there was hardly any time left for him to preach.

The pastor approached the worship leader and commended him for the quality of the worship, then explained that he desired the overall service to be a certain length of time. He went on to explain that in order to accommodate for the preaching of the Word, he wanted the worship part of the service to be kept to a set amount of time. The pastor expected the worship leader to gladly comply, and the pastor assumed that the excessive length was simply a failure on his part to communicate his expectations. The response he received shocked him! The worship leader said, "Listen, I'm in charge of the worship, and you're in charge of the preaching. Don't tell me how to lead worship, and I won't tell you how to preach."

Had the pastor known this person had such a rebellious and independent attitude, he would have never appointed him to lead worship in the first place. It's ideal for a pastor to know people well before placing them in key positions; haste in the selection process often produces regrettable results. A pastor takes a risk when he places someone of unproven character into a position of leadership. Talent and ability are great, but without the right attitude, a person can ultimately cause more problems than the benefits are worth.

There are people being born into the Body of Christ all the time who don't know how to properly respect and honor spiritual leaders. As a person of influence in the church, your submission—the respect and honor you show the pastor and those in authority—can and should be an example for others to follow.

Teamwork:
Relating Well to Other Leaders and to Coworkers

It's great and necessary to get along with the pastor, but it's not enough. As supportive ministers, we also need to get along well with our coworkers. We must demonstrate *submission* toward those *for whom* we work,

> A GOOD TEAM PLAYER GETS ALONG WELL WITH THE REST OF THE TEAM, NOT JUST WITH THE COACH.

and we need to have a sense of *teamwork* toward those *with whom* we work. A good team player gets along well with the rest of the team, not just with the coach. Individuals are not on a team to carry out their personal agendas. Teammates need to operate under the philosophy that "we" is more important than "me."

It is important that supportive ministers not be in competition with others, nor should we be territorial about our positions. It is also essential to respect and honor our coworkers and fellow staff members. Don't intrude inappropriately into their areas of responsibility. Practice the "Golden Rule" of doing unto others as you would have them do unto you (Matt. 7:12).

True success is not when you outshine others; true success is when the team functions at its full potential. President Franklin Roosevelt is reported to have said that what he wanted on his staff were young men with "a passion for anonymity." President Ronald Reagan had a plaque on his desk in the Oval Office that read, "There is no limit to what a man can do or where he can go if he doesn't mind who gets the credit." [1]

Ministry was never meant to be an extension of one's ego, but an expression of God's love. People who are struggling with insecurity and inferiority issues will often act defensively (being overly touchy) or offensively (being overly aggressive) toward others. Both of these behaviors undermine good working relationships and are detrimental to a positive work environment.

Occasionally, staff members compete over volunteers or church resources, selfishly grabbing for what will help their own department the most. They only see their area of responsibility; they don't see the big picture. However, each staff member should want to see all the departments of the church succeed, not just his own. One of the components of whether you had "plays well with others" checked on your first-grade report card was whether or not you were willing to share, and the necessity of sharing doesn't stop when you leave elementary school!

Make it your goal and aim to never be the troublemaker in a church, on a staff, or among a group of workers. Make it a priority to get along well with others and to be a peacemaker. Bring out the best in others. Live out what Paul said in Romans 12:18: "Do your part to live in peace with everyone, as much as possible" (*NLT*).

Diplomacy:
Relating Well to the Church Members

In addition to relating well to those in authority and to fellow-workers, supportive ministers must cultivate healthy working relationships with church members, especially those who work under their authority and supervision. This means that an effective supportive minister is going to need some skills in diplomacy. One of the definitions of the word "diplomacy" is *skill in handling affairs without arousing hostility*.[2]

Occasionally, a person allows a position or title to go to his head. In other words, his ministry position becomes something of a power trip and he becomes bossy, domineering, and offensive. Like King Rehoboam (see 2 Chronicles 10:1–16), he begins to deal harshly with the people and thereby alienate them. No matter how respectful a supportive minister is to the pastor, he will not ultimately be a blessing or an asset if he is continually creating "collateral damage" among the people and making messes that the pastor has to clean up.

Rehoboam's influence was drastically diminished because he lacked diplomacy and tact in dealing with people, and the saddest part is that he had been told by wise advisors exactly how to relate well to the people: *And they spoke to him, saying, "If you are kind to these people, and please them, and speak good words to them, they will be your servants forever"* (2 Chron. 10:7). The *Message* reads: "If you will be a servant to this people, be considerate of their needs and respond with compassion, work things out with them, they'll end up doing anything for you."

So often, we overlook the simple things such as treating people with kindness, courtesy, and respect. But if we're going to be successful, we can't ignore these fundamental and vital components of good people skills.

In discussing the reasons ministers fail, Gordon Lindsay said the following:

> "...one of the greatest causes of failure is the lack of thoughtfulness or tact. Many ministers have possessed

every qualification for service except this one. And why do they lack it? It is largely because they have not taken time to master it. Tact is thoughtfulness of others; it is sensitivity to the atmosphere of the moment; it is a combination of interest, sincerity, and brotherly love—giving the other fellow a sense of ease in one's presence. In a word, it is Christian love—the practice of the golden rule." [3]

Perhaps the best counsel ever given about getting along with others is found in First Corinthians chapter 13.

1 CORINTHIANS 13:1–7 (*Amplified*)

1 If I [can] speak in the tongues of men and [even] of angels, but have not love (that reasoning, intentional, spiritual devotion such as is inspired by God's love for and in us), I am only a noisy gong or a clanging cymbal.

2 And if I have prophetic powers (the gift of interpreting the divine will and purpose), and understand all the secret truths and mysteries and possess all knowledge, and if I have [sufficient] faith so that I can remove mountains, but have not love (God's love in me) I am nothing (a useless nobody).

3 Even if I dole out all that I have [to the poor in providing] food, and if I surrender my body to be burned or in order that I may glory, but have not love (God's love in me), I gain nothing.

4 Love endures long and is patient and kind; love never is envious nor boils over with jealousy, is not boastful or vainglorious, does not display itself haughtily.

5 It is not conceited (arrogant and inflated with pride); it is not rude (unmannerly) and does not act unbecomingly. Love (God's love in us) does not insist on its own rights or its own way, for it is not self-seeking; it is not touchy or fretful or resentful; it takes no account of the evil done to it [it pays no attention to a suffered wrong].

**6 It does not rejoice at injustice and unrighteousness,
but rejoices when right and truth prevail.**

**7 Love bears up under anything and everything that
comes, is ever ready to believe the best of every person,
its hopes are fadeless under all circumstances, and it
endures everything [without weakening].**

It doesn't matter how skilled or anointed we might be. If we can't walk in the love of God toward others, what are we really accomplishing? If we have great gifts of God's Spirit but are barren concerning the fruit of the Spirit, can we really please God? We must exhibit submission toward those in authority, teamwork toward those who are our coworkers, and diplomacy–love and goodwill–toward everyone in the Body of Christ.

When we "play well" with others, it goes a long way toward creating a healthy, enjoyable, and productive work environment. As author Kevin Lawson said:

> Long-term associate staff members report that supportive work relationships with their supervisor (normally the senior pastor) and with other associates on staff (if any) are among the keys to thriving in ministry. Healthy and supportive staff relationships can make ministry seem like heaven, even when ministry demands and stresses are high. But relationships with a supervisor or fellow associates that deteriorate into isolation, animosity, or indifference can take much of the joy out of even the best of ministry results.[4]

When you get along with your pastor, fellow supportive ministers, and church members even the stressful situations will be resolved in peace, and you will enjoy the fruit of being a great supportive minister.

QUESTIONS FOR REFLECTION AND DISCUSSION

1. Overall, do you "play well with others"?
2. How do you contribute to the joy of your pastor, other leaders, and coworkers?

3. Have you ever caused your leader grief or sorrow? How?
4. In what ways is the attitude you project toward your pastor and other leaders a good example of submission and respect?
5. Are you a compliant person—willing to yield? Or are you a self-willed person—adamant about doing everything your way?
6. Regarding your coworkers, are you competitive or cooperative?
7. Do you cultivate good relationships and bring out the best in others, or do you have a tendency to offend others?
8. How well do you personify the attributes of love described in First Corinthians chapter 13? Circles the response that best describes your personality:

   • I am patient.

Never	Sometimes	Usually	Always

   • I am kind.

Never	Sometimes	Usually	Always

   • I am not jealous.

Never	Sometimes	Usually	Always

   • I am not boastful.

Never	Sometimes	Usually	Always

   • I don't act arrogantly.

Never	Sometimes	Usually	Always

   • I am not rude.

Never	Sometimes	Usually	Always

   • I don't insist on my own way.

Never	Sometimes	Usually	Always

   • I am not touchy or easily hurt.

Never	Sometimes	Usually	Always

   • I am not resentful and don't hold grudges.

Never	Sometimes	Usually	Always

- I don't notice when other people treat me wrongly.

    Never   Sometimes   Usually   Always
- I only rejoice when right and truth prevail.

    Never   Sometimes   Usually   Always
- I bear up under anything that comes my way.

    Never   Sometimes   Usually   Always
- I believe the best of every person.

    Never   Sometimes   Usually   Always

9. If asked to fill out the previous survey for you, would your pastor/supervisor, coworkers, and fellow church members circle the same responses you did?
10. What did you learn from this chapter and how can you apply it?
11. What areas do you need to pray about or improve in?

---

[1] Selling Power Editors, "Ronald Reagan's Selling Power," *Selling Power*, January 1982, http://www.sellingpower.com/article/display.asp?print=TRUE&aid=sp835 4385.

[2] *Merriam-Webster's Collegiate Dictionary*, 11th ed., s.v. "Diplomacy."

[3] Gordon Lindsay, *The Charismatic Ministry* (Dallas: Christ for the Nations, Inc., 1983), 14.

[4] Reprinted from *How to Thrive in Associate Staff Ministry* by Kevin E. Lawson, with permission from the Alban Institute. Copyright © 2000 by The Alban Institute, Inc. All rights reserved.

Great Supportive Ministers Have a Servant's Heart

"You know that the rulers of the Gentiles lord it over them, and those who are great exercise authority over them.

Yet it shall not be so among you; but whoever desires to become great among you, let him be your servant.

And whoever desires to be first among you, let him be your slave—

just as the Son of Man did not come to be served, but to serve, and to give His life a ransom for many."

—Matthew 20:25–28

Jesus came to this earth to be a servant of mankind, and He commissioned us to serve as well. When Jesus prayed for His disciples He said to His Father God, *"As You sent Me into the world, I also have sent them into the world"* (John 17:18). When Jesus washed the feet of the disciples at the Last Supper, He said, *"If I then, your Lord and Teacher, have washed your feet, you also ought to wash one another's feet. For I have given you an example, that you should do as I have done to you. Most assuredly, I say to you, a servant is not greater than his master; nor is he who is sent greater than he who sent him. If you know these things, blessed are you if you do them"* (John 13:14–17).

Ministry is not about titles and positions. It is not about recognition and prestige. It is about serving others with the love of God. The highest commendation Paul gave Timothy may have been when he said, *"You know his proven character, that as a son with his father he served with me in the gospel"* (Phil. 2:22).

Occasionally, people in ministry lose their eagerness to serve and become very particular about what kind of work they're willing to do. They develop an attitude that they are "too good" to do certain tasks. We may have the privilege at times to specialize in serving in a particular area, but we should always be willing to do whatever it takes to get the overall job of ministry done. Instead of saying, "That's not my department [or area of expertise]," we ought to be willing to put our hand to any task that needs to be done in order to benefit the whole team.

'Too Good' to Serve?

Experienced pastors have learned to be very leery about people who seek authority, power, and control. Pastors know that those who are the greatest asset to the church are those who sim- ply seek to serve; they are not jockeying for position or pursuing prestige and recognition.

> ... THOSE WHO ARE THE GREATEST ASSET TO THE CHURCH ARE THOSE WHO SIMPLY SEEK TO SERVE.

In Luke chapter 14, Jesus told a parable that illustrated the kind of people who actively pursue recognition and contrasted this arrogant attitude with the kind of attitude we should adopt—one that is humble and allows other people to *bestow* recognition rather than our striving to be recognized.

LUKE 14:7–11

7   So [Jesus] told a parable to those who were invited, when He noted how they chose the best places, saying to them:

8 "When you are invited by anyone to a wedding feast, do not sit down in the best place, lest one more honorable than you be invited by him;

9 and he who invited you and him come and say to you, 'Give place to this man,' and then you begin with shame to take the lowest place.

10 But when you are invited, go and sit down in the lowest place, so that when he who invited you comes he may say to you, 'Friend, go up higher.' Then you will have glory in the presence of those who sit at the table with you.

11 For whoever exalts himself will be humbled, and he who humbles himself will be exalted."

People who truly have a servant's heart are pleased to serve behind the scenes and don't mind rolling up their sleeves and working hard. Since they are doing their work for the Lord, they aren't concerned whether anyone else notices what they are doing.

Consider the following statements:

• "I don't know what your destiny will be, but one thing I know: the only ones among you who will be really happy are those who will have sought and found how to serve."[1] (Albert Schweitzer)

• "The measure of a man is not how many servants he has but how many men he serves." [2] (Dwight L. Moody)

Seminary professor Leonard Sweet told the following story:

One of our students received an appointment from a bishop, and the student did not feel the placement exactly suited his abilities.

I overheard him complaining about it to another student, and then the other student said, "You know, the world's a better place because Michelangelo did not say, "I don't do ceilings."

Her comment stopped me dead in my tracks. I had to admit she was right.

If you and I are going to be faithful to the ministry God is calling us to, then we had better understand that. I reflected on the attitudes of key people throughout the Scriptures and the history of the Church.

The world's a better place because a German monk named Martin Luther did not say, "I don't do doors."

The world's a better place because an Oxford don named John Wesley didn't say, "I don't do preaching in fields."

"The world's a better place because Moses didn't say, "I don't do Pharaohs or mass migrations."

The world's a better place because Noah didn't say, "I don't do arks and animals."

The world's a better place because Rahab didn't say, "I don't do enemy spies."

The world's a better place because Ruth didn't say, "I don't do mothers-in-law."

The world's a better place because Samuel didn't say, "I don't do mornings."

The world's a better place because David didn't say, "I don't do giants."

The world's a better place because Peter didn't say, "I don't do Gentiles."

The world's a better place because John didn't say, "I don't do deserts."

The world's a better place because Mary didn't say, "I don't do virgin births."

The world's a better place because Paul didn't say, "I don't do correspondence."

The world's a better place because Mary Magdalene didn't say, "I don't do feet."

The world's a better place because Jesus didn't say, "I don't do crosses."

The world will be a better place only if you and I don't say, "I don't do..." [3]

What are the tasks that you've said, "I don't do..."? Are there any jobs that you consider "beneath you"? What tasks in the church aren't being done simply because people are unwilling to do them?

Remember, Jesus didn't come to be served, but to serve, and He commissioned us to do the same. Our goal should be to serve others the way Jesus did—with humility, love, and a servant's heart.

QUESTIONS FOR REFLECTION AND DISCUSSION

1. How are you demonstrating a servant's heart, or attitude, in your work for the Lord?
2. Are you willing to do whatever it takes to get the job done?
3. Do you serve others well? In what ways do you "wash the feet" of others?
4. Have you ever thought, That's not my job! when asked to do something?
5. Are there some things you feel you're "too good" to do?
6. Are you content to work behind the scenes and receive no recognition, or would you rather do more visible work that others notice?
7. What did you learn from this chapter and how can you apply it?
8. What areas do you need to pray about or improve in?

---

[1] Quoted in Ted Goodman, ed., *The Forbes Book of Business Quotations* (New York: Black Dog & Leventhal Publishers, 1997), 764.

[2] Mark Water, ed., *The New Encyclopedia of Christian Quotations* (Grand Rapids: Baker Books, 2000), 942.

[3] Leonard Sweet, "I Don't Do," *Sweetened*, http://www.leonardsweet.com/includes/ShowSweetenedArticles.asp?articleID=83.

Great Supportive Ministers Are Energetic and Enthusiastic

Imagine trying to lead a group of people who are apathetic, lethargic, listless, indifferent, and lackadaisical:

- Whenever you suggest something, they act sluggish and uninterested.
- They lack motivation and desire.
- They procrastinate and have the philosophy, "Never do today what you can put off until tomorrow."
- They are willing to barely plod along, like a snail or sloth, with a "whatever will be, will be" attitude.
- They don't put forth energy and are happy to coast on past momentum or on the efforts of others.
- They only want to do something if it's convenient, comfortable, and easy.
- They project the attitude, *I'll get to it if I can get to it, and if I ever do it, I'll exert the least amount of effort possible. And, I'll do it with just enough quality to get by.*

No leader likes to pull dead weight. A pastor wants every member of the team striving, contributing, and releasing energy together to get the job done. When team effort isn't taking place, Proverbs 10:26 becomes a reality: "Lazy people are a pain to their employer. They are like smoke in the eyes or vinegar that sets the teeth on edge" (*NLT*).

The Bible warns strongly against laziness and idleness.

PROVERBS 6:6–11 (*NLT*)

6   **Take a lesson from the ants, you lazybones. Learn from their ways and be wise!**

7   **Even though they have no prince, governor, or ruler to make them work,**

8   **they labor hard all summer, gathering food for the winter.**

9   **But you, lazybones, how long will you sleep? When will you wake up? I want you to learn this lesson:**

10 **A little extra sleep, a little more slumber, a little folding of the hands to rest—**

11 **and poverty will pounce on you like a bandit; scarcity will attack you like an armed robber.**

PROVERBS 26:13–16

13 **The lazy man says, "There is a lion in the road! A fierce lion is in the streets!"**

14 **As a door turns on its hinges, So does the lazy man on his bed.**

15 **The lazy man buries his hand in the bowl; It wearies him to bring it back to his mouth.**

16 **The lazy man is wiser in his own eyes Than seven men who can answer sensibly.**

These passages detail the actions and rewards of a lazy person. Can you imagine someone so lazy that when he eats he only has enough energy to put his hand into the bowl of food because he's too lazy to pull his hand back and put the food in his mouth? This is the sort of person who doesn't finish what he starts. He is not motivated enough to follow anything through to completion. The Bible says to this lazy man, "Poverty will pounce on you like a bandit; scarcity will attack you like an armed robber" (Prov. 6:11 *NLT*).

Pastors want supportive ministers who exhibit passion, zeal, eagerness, and enthusiasm in their work for the Lord.

They want people who are industrious and will bring energy to their work. They desire people who will carry out what Ecclesiastes 9:10 says: "Whatever

> NO LEADER LIKES TO PULL DEAD WEIGHT.

your hand finds to do, do it with all your might" (*NIV*). To borrow an old phrase, pastors desire workers who have "fire in their belly," meaning the workers have internal motivation and do not require constant babysitting, oversight, or motivation from other sources.

Jesus was referring directly to the works of the Laodicean church when He said, "I know all the things you do, that you are neither hot nor cold. I wish you were one or the other! But since you are like lukewarm water, I will spit you out of my mouth!" (Rev. 3:15–16 *NLT*). Jesus chastised the church for their ambivalent attitude. He wanted them to care one way or the other!

Whole-Hearted Effort

We've seen the behavior we're *not* supposed to have—lazy, apathetic, indifferent, and so forth. Now let's study the way we're *supposed* to serve as described in Romans 12:11:

- *"Not lagging in diligence, fervent in spirit, serving the Lord…"*
- "Never be lazy in your work, but serve the Lord enthusiastically" (*NLT*).
- "Don't burn out; keep yourselves fueled and aflame. Be alert servants of the Master" (*Message*).
- "Never lag in zeal and in earnest endeavor; be aglow and burning with the Spirit, serving the Lord" (*Amplified*).

There are many examples in the Bible where individuals rightly served with great diligence and vigor:

- The people following Nehemiah's leadership did their work with amazing efficiency because "…*the people had a mind to work*" (Neh. 4:6). The *New International Version* says, "…The people worked with all their heart."

- Paul said, "To this end I labor, struggling with all his energy, which so powerfully works in me" (Col.1:29 *NIV*).
- Apollos was described as being "fervent in spirit" (Acts 18:25).
- Epaphras was *"always laboring fervently...in prayers"* (Col. 4:12).
- James said that *"the effective, fervent prayer of a righteous man avails much"* and that Elijah "prayed earnestly" (James 5:16–17).

Are you laboring with energy and enthusiasm? Are you fervently working with your whole heart, or is your work marked by half-hearted effort?

There is an interesting story in the Old Testament that illustrates the problem of half-hearted effort. King Joash went to the prophet Elisha, and the prophet told the king to take some arrows and to strike them on the ground. When the king struck the ground three times Elisha became angry with him and said, *"You should have struck five or six times; then you would have struck Syria till you had destroyed it! But now you will strike Syria only three times"* (2 Kings 13:18–19).

It may seem unfair to us that Elisha rebuked the king when Elisha had not given Joash specific instructions on how many times to strike the ground. But the king's actions revealed his underlying attitude; he didn't respond with his whole heart, and Elisha knew that half-hearted effort would produce half-hearted results.

People who are full of energy and enthusiasm will do their work thoroughly and well. They have a strong work ethic, producing strong results. Proverbs 22:29 says, "Do you see any truly competent workers? They will serve kings rather than ordinary people" (*NLT*). Do you want to accomplish great things? Then become a motivated person, full of desire and enthusiasm. As Peter Drucker once said, "History has been written not by the most talented but by the most motivated."[1]

QUESTIONS FOR REFLECTION AND DISCUSSION

1. In what ways do you infuse your work for the Lord with energy and enthusiasm?
2. How often does someone or something have to motivate you in order for you to work more diligently?
3. Do you see yourself in any of the biblical admonitions concerning laziness or idleness?
4. Do you see yourself and your work ethic in the various translations of Romans 12:11?
5. If you had been King Joash, how many times would you have struck the arrows on the ground? Why?
6. What did you learn from this chapter and how can you apply it?
7. What areas do you need to pray about or improve in?

---

[1] Robert D. Dale, *Surviving Difficult Church Members* (Nashville: Abingdon Press, 1984), 99.

CHAPTER 21

Great Supportive Ministers Are Balanced

Repose is as needful to the mind as sleep to the body...

If we do not rest...we shall break down.

Even the earth must lie fallow and have her Sabbaths, and so must we.

Hence the wisdom and compassion of our Lord, when he said to his disciples, "Let us go into the desert and rest awhile."

–Charles Spurgeon, *Lectures to My Students*

In the previous chapter, we established the importance of being an energetic and enthusiastic worker. However, there is more to success in supportive ministry (and in life) than simply being a hard worker. Work cannot be the only thing in our life. We must develop and maintain dimensions of our life as well. *Balance* is a vital key to being physically and emotionally healthy *and* to experiencing longevity in the ministry.

In his book *The Rhythm of Life*, Richard Exley explained that we all of have a need for harmony and balance in four areas of life: *worship, work, rest,* and *play* [1]. It's commendable to have a great work ethic, but if we're not careful, we can easily rob ourselves in the other areas of life.

When serving in ministry it's especially easy to justify over-working ourselves, because we deem our tasks to be noble and commendable. After all, it's God's work that we're doing! But instead of living in peace as God intended, we can end up feeling pressured all the time.

> GOD WANTS US TO WORK HARD AND BE INDUSTRIOUS, BUT HE DOESN'T WANT US TO BE WORKAHOLICS...

I like the conclusion to which one formerly-compulsive person came: "I've come to the realization that when I die, my in-box will be full." Realizing that no matter how much work he accomplished there was always going to be more work to do, this man finally chose to be at peace with what he was able to accomplish and to not allow himself to get uptight about the rest.

Ministers who lack balance in their lives are strong candidates for burnout. Dr. Frank Minirth and Dr. Paul Meier say that burnout results from "bearing pressure and strain so intense that they consume our inner-resources." Burnout has been called "the problem of good intentions." According to Minirth and Meier, those who will suffer from burnout are "leaders who have never been able to accept limitations. They are those who have pushed themselves too hard for too long." [2]

Take Time to Invest in Yourself

God wants us to work hard and be industrious, but He doesn't want us to be workaholics—obsessed and consumed with working. Life and ministry aren't all about *output*. We must have quality *input* as well. Someone once said, "If your outgo exceeds your income, your upkeep becomes your downfall." That's true in all areas of life, not just in the area of finances. Some people feel guilty if they are doing anything other than producing, but we all need to take time to invest in ourselves and replenish our inner-resources if we're going to be able to produce in the long run.

Paul told Timothy, *"Take heed to yourself"* (1 Tim. 4:16). If you don't take care of yourself, no one else will! Paul went on to tell Timothy that God *"gives us richly all things to enjoy"* (1 Tim. 6:17). Be sure to take time to enjoy the good things of life. Develop wholesome activities and hobbies that relax you and supply you with much-needed mental diversion and refreshing.

In Philippians chapter 2, the Apostle Paul describes a young minister named Epaphroditus who almost died through overwork (Phil. 2:25–30). Verse 30 says that Epaphroditus was *"not regarding his life."* The *Wuest* translation renders that same verse, "He recklessly exposed his life."

There are natural consequences to "not regarding our life." We need to avoid recklessness and take heed to how we care for our physical body—even in working for the Lord. Jesus Himself believed in resting and pacing oneself in ministry.

MARK 6:31–32

31 And He said to them, "Come aside by yourselves to a deserted place and rest a while." For there were many coming and going, and they did not even have time to eat.

32 So they departed to a deserted place in the boat by themselves.

You will be a greater asset to your pastor and your church if you keep yourself refreshed and are able to contribute over the long haul. It is far better to pace yourself than to continually keep your nose to the grindstone and then burn out prematurely.

Where Do We Need Balance?

So far in this chapter, we've seen that we need to balance physical labor with physical rest. Where else do we need balance in our lives? First, we need *proper balance in our priorities*. Family is a major priority—our marriage and our children should not take second place to the ministry. After our family, our work and service to the church follows. All of these are important; balance is achieved when we give each its appropriate attention.

> IT IS FAR BETTER TO PACE YOURSELF THAN TO CONTINUALLY KEEP YOUR NOSE TO THE GRINDSTONE AND THEN BURN OUT PREMATURELY.

This issue of imbalance between work and family is mainly a problem for those who have a tendency to focus on work at the expense of everything else. However, there are those on the opposite end of the spectrum who focus so much on everything else that they have no time for work or service. Some people are so busy working for God that they neglect the needs of their spouse and their children. Others are so focused on family and fun that they never have any time for church or to serve God. Neither extreme is pleasing to God.

Will you really be considered a success in ministry if your spouse and children end up resenting God and the church because you disregarded them and failed to meet their needs in your quest to become a great minister? God did not call ministers to sacrifice their spouse or children on the altar of Christian service. The witness and work of some ministers have been undermined because of their neglecting the natural responsibilities of life. While trying to excel in spiritual matters, some have been remiss in paying bills, and other aspects of the home life have been in disarray. This ought not to be.

When we seek balance in our priorities concerning work and family, we will successfully minister to our spouse, our children, *and* to others.

Proper Balance
Between Tasks and Relationships

We've studied the need for proper balance in our priorities. Second, we must maintain *balance between tasks and relationships*.

Some supportive ministers are so relationship-oriented that they spend all their time at church chatting, fellowshipping, and visiting with others. As a result, they neglect the work they have volunteered or are paid to do. Other supportive ministers are so focused on their tasks that they come across as cold and uncaring to people. Both of these are unbalanced approaches to tasks and relationships. Our aim is somewhere in the middle.

We can give ample attention to the people we work with and minister to at church while also giving ample attention to the necessary tasks at hand. Tasks and relationships are both important. If there were no people at our church, there would be no job—but if we don't do our job, there may be no people! We must strive to balance the two.

Proper Balance
Between the Natural and the Spiritual

First, we need proper balance in our priorities. Second, we must maintain balance between tasks and relationships. Third, we must strike a *balance between the natural and the spiritual.*

It's been said that some people are so heavenly-minded they're no earthly good, and others are so earthly-minded they're no heavenly good. God wants us to be attentive and alert in both the spiritual and natural realms.

One pastor related that he had a youth minister on his staff who only wanted to focus on the spiritual side of things. This youth minister wanted to stay home and pray all the time instead of spending time with the youth. The pastor valued prayer but not at the expense of building relationships with and ministering to the youth.

Proper Balance
Between Seriousness and Humor

Do you have proper balance in your priorities? Are you maintaining balance between the tasks you are required to complete and the relationships that require nurturing? Have you reached a balance between the natural and the spiritual aspects of ministry? Do you have a proper *balance between seriousness and humor*?

Some people really need to lighten up and enjoy life; they need to stop taking themselves so seriously. (People who are moody and disagreeable are not at all pleasant to be around.) Others need to realize that life is not all fun and games—there are times to stop joking and to get serious. The ideal supportive minister finds a healthy balance between the two and knows the appropriate time for each.

One of the great lessons I learned about balance came while I was coaching my son's basketball team back when he was in the third grade. I grew up in Indiana, so basketball was a big deal to me, but I had determined that I was not going to be too intense with the young boys on my team. Sure, I wanted them to learn the basics of the game and to do well when we played, but I was determined not to be hard on the kids and not to make winning and losing a life-or-death situation. I wanted the kids to have fun while they were learning and playing the game.

I think I did pretty well balancing those objectives throughout the year, and even though I'm a competitive person, I endeavored not to make the atmosphere too intense for the kids. However, when it came to the last game of the season—the championship game—I found myself getting very intense. I wasn't *outwardly* out of control (I wasn't screaming or going berserk), but *inwardly* I felt myself getting uptight and really, really, really wanting to win.

We were down to the last fifteen seconds of regulation, and it was a one-point game. I called a time-out and diagrammed three plays for our team. I drew an out-of-bounds play and then two different defensive set-ups based on whether or not we scored on that first offensive play. After going over the three options, I asked the boys if anyone had any questions. I felt a tug on my left sleeve, and I looked over at one of my players. "What is it?" I asked, expecting a question about one of the plays I had just shown the team. The player looked up at me and said, "My dog had puppies."

I smiled and immediately realized that I was taking the game *way* too seriously. I had great kids on my team, but none of them cared about the game nearly as much as I did. That young boy's comment broke the tension I was feeling, and it helped me to see that other people have different perspectives on life than I do—and that each person's perspective is as important to him as mine is to me.

I later thought of this experience in terms of ministry. Those who go to church and even those who work in the church are all at various levels of commitment and intensity. If I want to be successful in ministry, I have to acknowledge that truth and to work with people based on where *they* are.

It's great to have high standards and to encourage people to be committed, but we can't drive people so hard and set expectations so high that it discourages all but the most stalwart volunteers. We need balance in our personal lives and in working with others.

Remember, balance is a vital key to being physically and emotionally healthy *and* to experiencing longevity in ministry. Examine Exley's four areas of life—worship, work, rest, and play—and see how balanced you are. Take some time to straighten out any priorities that may be out of order and to address any possible imbalances in your life.

QUESTIONS FOR REFLECTION AND DISCUSSION

1. Do you have a healthy balance between these four areas of life: worship, work, rest, and play?
2. In what areas are you overdoing it? What areas need more attention?
3. Are you a workaholic who is neglecting other vital areas of your life? If so, how can you correct that tendency?

4. How are your "inner-resources?" Are you ministering from an overflow, or are you dealing with burnout?
5. List five hobbies or activities that help you take your mind off work.
6. When was the last time you engaged in each of these activities you listed?
7. What steps do you take to balance yourself in the Work/Family area?
8. How balanced are you in Tasks/Relationships?
9. How do you maintain your balance between the Natural and the Spiritual?
10. How balanced are you in Seriousness/Humor?
11. What did you learn from this chapter and how can you apply it?
12. What areas do you need to pray about or improve in?

---

[1] Richard Exley, *The Rhythm of Life* (Tulsa: Honor Books, 1987), 11–15.

[2] Herbert J. Freudenberger, *Burnout: The High Cost of High Achievement* (Garden City, New York: Doubleday, 1980), 11–12.

Great Supportive Ministers Are Flexible and Growth-Oriented

Even if you're on the right track, you'll get run over if you just sit there.

–Will Rogers

G reat staff members maintain flexibility and pliability in their lives. They don't get stagnant and stuck in a rut. The words of a dying church (also the words of a supportive minister who is in the process of becoming outdated) are, "We've never done it that way before."

What are the traits of growth-oriented, flexible people?

• They are life-long learners.
• They are willing to address and overcome weaknesses their life.
• They are open to new ideas and new ways of doing things.
• They adjust graciously to unexpected developments.
• They adapt to other people.
• They are willing to embrace new assignments or relinquish old roles for the good of the church.
• They continually seek improvement.
• They experience spiritual vitality in their life.

In the rest of this chapter we will look at each of these traits in more detail and study how they impact the effectiveness of supportive ministers.

Life-Long Learners

Life-long learners are not content with what they learned years ago; they are always looking to learn new things. They're especially hungry for information that will enable them to stay on the cutting edge in their area of ministry. Certain principles are eternal, but technology, methods, and style issues are continually changing. As a result, this type of supportive minister reads appropriate magazines and journals, attends continuing education seminars, and interacts with others in his field to stay abreast of the latest developments. By continually learning and improving their skills, life-long learners become more and more valuable to the organization.

Willing to Address
and Overcome Weaknesses

These supportive ministers do not consider themselves to be omniscient or infallible, nor do they have a "know-it-all" attitude. When the pastor or their supervisor brings correction, they receive the information graciously. Instead of taking it as a personal attack and becoming defensive, they welcome it as an opportunity to grow and improve.

Open to New Ideas and
New Ways of Doing Things

There is a temptation for people to get in a "comfort zone" and to just keep doing the same things over and over. After all, it's easier that way and it doesn't present any challenges or require any potentially painful changes.

Have you gotten into a rut with your routine? Are you open to new ideas, even if they require you to leave your current comfort zone? The old way of doing things may be the most familiar way, but it isn't necessarily the best way.

Sometimes old programs just need to be revitalized–they can be salvaged but they need a face-lift. Yet other old programs need to be

> THERE IS A TEMPTATION FOR PEOPLE TO GET IN A "COM-FORT ZONE" AND TO JUST KEEP DOING THE SAME THINGS OVER AND OVER.

replaced altogether. As one person said, "If you always do what you've always done, you'll always be what you've always been."

Adjusts Graciously to Unexpected Developments

Things change and surprises happen. The unpredictable often occurs, demanding that we think on our feet, so to speak. Sometimes we are required to make immediate adjustments because of changes that take place. When immediate adjustments are required, some people get busy and make the adjustments while others get flustered and panic. There is an old saying that every supportive minister should take to heart: "He that is flexible shall not get bent out of shape."

Adapts to Other People

One of the great skills the Apostle Paul demonstrated in ministry was that of adapting to other people. In First Corinthians 9:22 he said, *"...I have become all things to all men."* The adaptability Paul exhibited was not because he was a weak person who lacked personal convictions or fortitude; rather, Paul's adaptability was a strength he used to accomplish great results for God's Kingdom. Paul was not a rigid, inflexible person. While he never wavered from his godly principles, Paul made whatever changes he could in order to get the job done.

Willing to Embrace New Assignments or Relinquish Old Roles for the Good of the Church

These supportive ministers are not afraid of new endeavors. They are willing to let go of the security of the old and embrace the adventure of the new. They don't have their ego and identity wrapped up in a title or position, so they are willing to step into an entirely new role if that will better serve God's Kingdom and the local church.

Continually Seeks Improvement

These supportive ministers are never content with the status quo. They are always looking for ways to be more effective and productive. They're thankful for the people they've reached, but they want to reach more. They are open to innovations and changes that will take programs and projects to a new level. Great supportive ministers continually seek to improve both personally and professionally.

Experiences Spiritual Vitality

These supportive ministers do not live off an old experience; their relationship with God is up-to-date and vibrant. Their devotional life (Bible study and prayer) is strong, and the fruit of the Spirit is abounding in their life. They sense God's pruning work in their life (John 15:1–4; Heb. 12:5–11), and they are being changed and transformed by the Spirit of God (Rom. 12:1–2; 2 Cor. 3:18).

While changes is sometimes painful, it hurts less when we're flexible. Growth-oriented supportive ministers are forward-looking, forward-thinking, and forward-moving. They believe the best is yet to come and are eager to reach their full potential.

QUESTIONS FOR REFLECTION AND DISCUSSION

1. Are you a life-long learner? How are you staying on the cutting edge in your area of ministry?
2. Are you willing to address and overcome weaknesses in your life? Do you receive correction graciously, or do you feel threatened and become defensive when someone corrects you?

3. Are you open to new ideas and new ways of doing things? Do you see changes as a threat, or as an opportunity?
4. List some new ideas you have embraced and put into practice recently (in any area of your life).
5. How do react to and handle unexpected developments?
6. In what ways have you adapted yourself to coworkers?
7. Are you willing to embrace new assignments and relinquish old roles for the good of the church?
8. Do you continually seek to improve your personal life and your area(s) of ministry responsibility?
9. Are you experiencing spiritual vitality in your life? Is your relationship with God up-to-date?
10. What did you learn from this chapter and how can you apply it?
11. What areas do you need to pray about or improve in?

Great Supportive Ministers Are Internally Motivated

The Apostle Paul was overwhelmed by the Macedonian believers' initiative to respond to the Christians in Jerusalem who were in need. Paul had it on his heart to provide financial relief to the Jerusalem believers, and he had been trying to motivate various churches to participate in giving. The Macedonians not only rose to the challenge, but far exceeded Paul's expectations. Instead of half-heartedly complying with Paul's request, they responded whole-heartedly and became vessels of God's grace in an overflowing and dynamic way.

2 CORINTHIANS 8:3–5 (*The Living Bible*)
3 **They gave not only what they could afford, but far more; and I can testify that they did it because they wanted to, and not because of nagging on my part.**
4 **They begged us to take the money so they could share in the joy of helping the Christians in Jerusalem.**
5 **Best of all, they went beyond our highest hopes....**

Verse 5 in the *Message* reads, "This was totally spontaneous, entirely their own idea, and caught us completely off guard. What explains it was that they had first given themselves unreservedly to God and to us. The other giving simply flowed out of the purposes of God working in their lives."

As Paul was writing this letter to the Corinthian church, telling them how wonderfully other believers had given to the cause, I'm sure he hoped that the Corinthians would get the hint and give as well.

Psalm 110:3 says, "Thy people will *volunteer freely* in the day of Thy power..." (*NASB*). It must have brought tremendous joy to Paul's heart to see believers step forward and participate so eagerly in helping others. One of the great-

> ONE OF THE GREATEST JOYS AND SATISFACTIONS A LEADER HAS IS WHEN THOSE AROUND HIM ARE MOTIVATED FROM WITHIN.

est joys and satisfactions a leader has is when those around him are motivated from within. No supervisor enjoys having to stay after people to make sure they do their work. No pastor wants to feel like the only way things will get done is if he continues to apply pressure.

A supervisor will often help a worker to set goals, but what a joy it is when the worker then meets or exceeds those goals on his own—because he was internally motivated to strive for excellence and success.

Anyone whose only motivators are to get a paycheck, to meet a minimum production quota, or to merely *maintain* a position will never be a peak performer. It's important to have a higher standard within you than what others may place upon you. Jesus introduced the concept of going the extra mile, when He said, "If a soldier demands that you carry his gear for a mile, carry it two miles" (Matt. 5:41 *NLT*).

William Barclay provided the following commentary about Jesus' statement in Matthew chapter 5:

> Palestine was an occupied country. At any moment a Jew might feel the touch of the flat of a Roman spear on his shoulder, and know that he was compelled to serve the Romans, it might be in the most menial way. That, in fact, is what happened to Simon of Cyrene, when he was compelled...to bear the cross of Jesus.

So, then, what Jesus is saying is: "Suppose your masters come to you and compel you to be a guide or a porter for a mile, don't do a mile with bitter and obvious resentment; go two miles with cheerfulness and with a good grace." What Jesus is saying is: "Don't be always thinking of your liberty to do as you like; be always thinking of your duty and your privilege to be of service to others. When a task is laid on you, even if the task is unreasonable and hateful, don't do it as a grim duty to be resented; do it as a service to be gladly rendered."

There are always two ways of doing things. A man can do the irreducible minimum and not a stroke more; he can do it in such a way as to make it clear that he hates the whole thing; he can do it with the barest minimum of efficiency and no more; or he can do it with a smile, with a gracious courtesy, with a determination, not only to do this thing, but to do it well and graciously. He can do it, not simply as well as he has to, but far better than anyone has any right to expect him to.[1]

Great supportive ministers are willing to go the extra mile—not because they are made to and not even because they are asked to, but because they have a heart to serve and *want* to.

Be a Self-Starter

Part of being internally motivated means being a self-starter. In other words, you know how to inspire yourself to do a good job and don't have to wait for someone else to motivate you. You don't wait until you are asked to do something; you see what needs to be done and take the initiative to go ahead and do it.

A staff member in one church told me that he felt part of his job was to see things that needed to be done and to handle them before the pastor ever became aware that something needed to be done. The ability to anticipate what needs to be done is a valuable asset. It's far better to minister and serve *proactively* and not merely *reactively*. In other words, it's better to anticipate and plan well rather than to neglect planning and to end up being in constant crisis-mode. The solution: plan your work then work your plan.

It's been said, "There are three types of people in life: those who make things happen, those who watch things happen, and those who aren't really sure what happened." Be a person who makes things happen! Don't only be motivated from within, but motivate and inspire those around you as well.

Initiative and Amenability

Taking initiative and being a self-starter doesn't mean a supportive minister doesn't have to maintain responsibility and accountability. We must find a balance between *initiative* and *amenability*. An amenable person is easy to be led, governable, and one who answers to another. If a supportive minister has too much initiative and not enough amenability, he will be overly aggressive, intrude into areas assigned to others, spend money that's not been approved, and fail to get permission before launching certain projects. On the other hand, a supportive minister who has too little initiative and too much amenability will never overstep his bounds, but neither will he do anything—*anything*—unless he's specifically told to do it.

Both of these extremes create problems for pastors and supervisors; therefore, we need to have a good blend of both initiative and amenability. This means that we're insightful enough to see what needs to be done and motivated enough to accomplish it (within the context of what is proper for us to do). At the same time, however, we remain submitted to authority and obtain authorization when it's appropriate. A wise supportive minister knows which tasks require special permission and which ones should simply be carried out within the scope of his assigned duties.

Some supportive ministers are internally motivated but because they haven't developed the other traits of great supportive ministers (such as loyalty, honesty, and so forth), their internal motivation drives them to do things contrary to the pastor's vision or desires. For initiative and internal motivation to be a blessing, we must balance it with continued responsibility and accountability and all the other positive traits that make a great supportive minister.

QUESTIONS FOR REFLECTION AND DISCUSSION

1. In what way are you internally motivated? In what way are you a self-starter?
2. What are some recent tasks that you carried out without having to be told to do them?
3. Do you delight in exceeding the goals set for you by others by creating even higher ones for yourself?
4. Do you go the extra mile or do the bare minimum?
5. Do you anticipate what needs to be done, or do you merely react to whatever comes up? Are you more proactive or reactive?
6. How do you balance initiative and amenability in your work?
7. What did you learn from this chapter and how can you apply it?
8. What areas do you need to pray about or improve in?

---

[1] William Barclay, *The Gospel of Matthew: Volume 1*, rev. ed. (Philadelphia: Westminster Press, 1975), 168–169.

Great Supportive Ministers Are Good Communicators

Then those who feared the Lord talked often one to another.

–Malachi 3:16 (*Amplified*)

Just because a person likes to talk doesn't mean he is a good communicator. As a matter of fact, good communication doesn't begin with talking or expressing one's self; it starts with being attentive to others, being a good observer, and listening well when other people speak. Once a person has accurately gathered all of the appropriate information, then and only then can it be processed, organized, and conveyed accurately.

The Apostle Paul's excellent powers of observation were part of what made him such an effective communicator. When Luke recorded Paul's ministry in Athens, he made special note of how Paul took time to observe the people and their religious practices (Acts 17:16–23). Before Paul spoke, he studied and examined the situation carefully. Paul's attention to detail is clearly seen in his statement, "For while I was passing through and examining the objects of your worship..." (Acts 17:23 *NASB*).

Jesus is another example of a minister who only spoke after spending time observing the people to whom He would minister. Yes, Jesus ministered from divine revelation, but His teaching was also influenced by His keen sense of observation.

> JUST BECAUSE A PERSON LIKES TO TALK DOESN'T MEAN HE IS A GOOD COMMUNICATOR.

Jesus' remarks about the widow's mite came after "He sat down opposite the treasury, and began observing how the multitude were putting money into the treasury" (Mark 12:41 *NASB*).

Scripture reveals that good communicators get the facts before they speak:

- *Ahimaaz was determined to run as a courier to the king even though he did not have all the necessary information. As a result, he was asked to step aside* (2 Sam. 18:19–30).
- Proverbs 18:13 says, *"He who answers a matter before he hears it, It is folly and shame to him."* The *Message* says, "Answering before listening is both stupid and rude."
- James said that we should be quick to listen and slow to speak (James 1:19 *NIV*).

It's not enough to provide information. Your information must be correct and you must supply that information to the correct people. Providing the right information to the right people is a vital part of a supportive minister's responsibilities. Consider the biblical precedents for this type of communication:

- The twelve spies in the Old Testament came back to report their findings (Num. 13:26–33; 14:6–10).
- Having been sent out by Jesus to minister, the disciples reported back to Jesus. Luke 9:10 says, "When the apostles returned, they reported to Jesus what they had done..." (*NIV*). The *New American Standard Bible* says, "They gave an account to Him of all that they had done...."
- Paul reported back after his missionary journeys. Acts 15:4 says, *"And when they had come to Jerusalem, they were*

*received by the church and the apostles and the elders; and they
reported all things that God had done with them."* (See also
Acts 14:27; 21:18–19.)

• Paul received reports from Timothy, Titus, and others
(Phil. 1:19; 1 Thess. 3:6; 2 Cor. 7:5–7).

In these biblical examples we see the following principles
in demonstration:

• We must provide information.
• The information we provide must be correct and in full.
• We must supply that correct information to the right per-
son or people.
• The way in which we communicate the correct informa-
tion is also important.

Therefore, to be an effective communicator as a supportive
minister, you must know who to report to, what type of information your supervisor needs from you, and the appropriate
way to communicate this necessary information. Some pastors
and supervisors want highly detailed information; others just
want the bottom line. If you're uncertain about which your
supervisor prefers, just ask. Your supervisor can tell you if he
wants you to provide more or fewer details in your reports. If
you are still uncertain at any given time, it's better to err on
the side of providing *too much* information than not enough.

Practical Tips to Better
Your Communication

Always make it a point to be accurate, specific, and con-
cise in your communication. If you are given instructions
about an assignment, it can be helpful to ask your supervisor
some clarifying questions to make sure you know exactly what
is expected of you. A typical clarifying question would be
something like this: "I understand that you're asking me to do
X, Y, and Z by such and such date. Is that correct?" With this
type of question, you are making sure that you understand the

scope of the assignment and are clarifying the deadline associated with it.

Depending on how involved the project is, it can also be very helpful to follow up the conversation in which the project was assigned by submitting a written summary to your supervisor, detailing what you understood his verbal assignment to be. This enables your supervisor to qualify and clarify any misunderstandings you might have or to give additional information you might need. On larger projects, written progress reports (periodic updates on how things are coming along) can be very helpful in keeping your supervisor and other members of the team up-to-date on your progress.

As an associate pastor, I kept a log of all the church members I ministered to and interacted within a given week, including brief details of what each situation or conversation entailed. Then I submitted this report each Friday to the senior pastor. Every person on the pastoral staff submitted similar types of reports to the senior pastor. In this way, we supportive ministers were able to function as the ears and eyes of the senior pastor, enabling him to further his scope of ministry beyond what he alone could do as an individual.

While the information in our reports was treated with great confidentiality, it was of enormous value in helping the team to function efficiently and effectively. Of course, there may be especially sensitive information that is not appropriate to share at various staff meetings but is only appropriate to share with the senior pastor or select staff members. That kind of information should not be included in general reports that may possibly be read by every staff member and should only be shared on a "need-to-know" basis.

It is it essential for a leadership team to communicate well. Proverbs 27:23 says, *"Be diligent to know the state of your flocks, And attend to your herds."* This can only happen if the appropriate information is being shared among the appropriate people. The left hand not knowing what the right hand is doing may be wonderful when it comes to the giving of alms (Matt. 6:3–4), but it's an invitation to chaos, inefficiency, and frustration when it comes to running an organization.

QUESTIONS FOR REFLECTION AND DISCUSSION

1. Are you attentive? Are you observant?
2. When given an assignment, do you listen carefully the first time, or do you have to go back and ask for repeated instructions afterwards?
3. Does your supervisor come to you and ask about the status or progress of various assignments, or do you keep the supervisor so well-informed that he never has to approach you?
4. When you are receiving instructions and assignments, what kind of questions do you ask to make sure you're hearing accurately and receiving all the information you need to do your job properly?
5. Do you know how much information and what type of information your pastor and/or supervisor wants in your reports?
6. Are you providing too much or too little information? Are you providing too many details or not enough?
7. What did you learn from this chapter and how can you apply it?
8. What areas do you need to pray about or improve in?

CHAPTER 25

Great Supportive Ministers Multiply Themselves

I'd rather get ten men to do the job than to do the job of ten men.

—Dwight L. Moody

Paul instructed Timothy, *"And the things that you have heard from me among many witnesses, commit these to faithful men who will be able to teach others also"* (2 Tim. 2:2). Paul understood the principle of multiplication. It's great when one person can do a job well; it's even better when he can motivate and inspire other people to serve, train them, and release them into productive roles in the ministry.

In the early days of your work as a supportive minister you will most likely focus on "doing ministry." However, with greater maturity and development, you will very likely begin to focus more on "developing ministers." In doing so, you must function as a good follower to your leader(s), and you must also cultivate and implement your own leadership skills.

A Scenario of Minister Multiplication

For example, let's say that a person in a church becomes an assistant to the pastor. This person's main areas of responsibility are hospital and nursing home visitation, praying with people who respond to the altar call at church services, and teaching the adult Sunday school class. For the first season of his involvement, this person does all these things by himself. After some time passes, he begins to realize that he could use some help in these areas. Besides having help to carry the load, he realizes that by sharing the work, he will afford other people the opportunity to share in the privilege of ministry.

This supportive minister must now transition from merely being a *doer of ministry* to becoming a *developer of ministers*. No longer is he merely carrying out ministry on an individual basis, but he will now begin equipping others to carry out ministry.

> THIS SUPPORTIVE MINISTER MUST NOW TRANSITION FROM MERELY BEING A *DOER OF MINISTRY* TO BECOMING A *DEVELOPER OF MINISTERS.*

In one scenario, he might start by recruiting a couple of assistant teachers and training them on how to teach the Sunday school class. He could then periodically have them substitute for him. Eventually, he might suggest to the pastor that the one class (especially if it has grown in numbers) be divided into two groups, with each of the assistants becoming a lead teacher over one group. The supportive minister could then oversee and assist the two new teachers as they continue to increase their skills and gain experience.

Concerning the other two areas of his responsibility (visitation and altar ministry), the supportive minister could select certain people and invite them to become part of either a Visitation Team or a Prayer Team. He could train them and ultimately release them to work in these important areas. He might still handle some of the visitation himself, especially in more critical situations, but now his major work will be done *through* others that he has trained and will now supervise.

By training others to carry out the work, this assistant minister has begun to delegate his responsibilities. Here are some important tips to keep in mind when it comes to delegating:

- Determine the areas in which your pastor/supervisor is comfortable with your delegating tasks and the areas in which he prefers for you to personally carry out the tasks.
- Before you delegate responsibility, develop proficiency in that area yourself. It's difficult to train someone in an area when you yourself lack competence. This principle applies when you are skilled or trained in an area and have been asked or need to recruit someone for the job who may have lesser training and experience than you do. This does not necessarily apply when you are recruiting or hiring someone to carry out a specific task and that person already has expertise that you do not possess. (For example, you may need to hire someone to install audio/video systems and there is no way you can be proficient in that area in order to train the installation person. In that case, you can simply obtain a professional to do the work you are not able, required, or expected to do.)
- When you recruit people to work with you and for you, it's good to tell them upfront what is expected of them in that particular area of responsibility. Furthermore, it is helpful for them to work alongside you for a season and observe you carrying out the tasks they will eventually perform. Later, as you continue to work together, the roles can be reversed—they can perform the task while you observe them, giving them feedback and further instructions as necessary. Finally, they will be trained and equipped and confident to do the work on their own.
- It's important to find the balance between not delegating enough responsibility and delegating too much responsibility.
- Realize that there is a difference between *delegating* and *abdicating*. Assuming that you have ongoing supervisory responsibilities, don't just tell people to do things and then never check up on them. Delegating involves elements of continuing oversight and awareness. This means

you ought to periodically evaluate the performance and results of those to whom you've delegated, and you ought to also provide them periodic feedback on their performance.

- For follow-up to be handled effectively there must be original objectives for the position/assignment with clearly-stated goals. (Otherwise, how would you as a supervisor know if your workers are doing a good job? How would you measure their job performance?)

- Oversight entails both praise and correction—commending and encouraging people for the areas in which they are doing well and addressing areas that need to be improved or corrected.

- Oversight and periodic evaluation is not the same as micromanaging, or continually looking over the person's shoulder and smothering them. While your involvement may be more intense with a new trainee, eventually you will provide oversight in a way that ensures quality but provides the person enough "breathing room" to work.

- People who are perfectionists often have trouble delegating. They may think no one will do the job as well as they will. That type of thinking is problematic in many ways. We must keep in mind that we didn't do all of our tasks perfectly the first time. We all made some mistakes, and we've got to be willing to allow others to make mistakes too. Besides, how will people ever grow and develop if they're not allowed to try? Actually performing the task (hands-on involvement) is the best method of learning.

- Delegation is not a magic wand you can wave in order instantly unload your responsibilities onto someone else. Delegation is never instant. There should be ample time for necessary training, follow-up, and ongoing mentoring or oversight. With delegating, you should have an ongoing interest in seeing the recipient of that assignment develop as a supportive minister and as a person.

- Serving God is a great honor, and faithfulness in serving Him is one of the great keys to the development of our character. Be sure that you take an interest in the spiritual development of the people to whom you delegate. Don't fall into the trap of simply having a utilitarian view of delegation—merely using people as a means of accomplishing tasks. What happens in a person's life when they serve God is just as important as the result of the person's work—if not more important! Keep both the spiritual and natural results in mind as you multiply yourself through others.
- There are limits to delegation. Everyone can't be the boss and not everyone can delegate. We'd have absolute chaos if everyone tried to delegate their duties to someone else and no one wanted to do the actual work. While there is wisdom in delegating, there is also honor in carrying out the work.

The idea of a leader multiplying himself through the involvement of others is nothing new. That's what Moses did in Exodus chapter 18. It's also what Jesus did with His own disciples. Jesus first called the twelve to come alongside Him—to listen and observe. He taught them and eventually provided periodic opportunities to put into practice what they had been seeing and learning. Eventually, Jesus left them with the full responsibility of the work. After properly training and equipping them, Jesus told the disciples, *"...As the Father has sent Me, I also send you"* (John 20:21).

QUESTIONS FOR REFLECTION AND DISCUSSION

1. How much of your effort is spent doing ministry and how much is spent developing others for ministry? Is the ratio (between doing and developing) what it should be?
2. If you feel you should be delegating to and developing others more than you are, what obstacles are standing in your way?

3. What are some specific ways you can begin to develop and equip others for ministry?

4. What kind of training do you provide for the people to whom you delegate responsibility?

5. How do you clearly communicate the job objectives and goals when you delegate?

6. How do you conduct follow-up with your workers to evaluate their performance and ensure that job goals are being met?

7. Have you ever allowed a sense of perfectionism to keep you from delegating to others? Give an example.

8. Do you have a utilitarian view of delegation? Is delegation merely a tool to help you accomplish more tasks? If so, what can you do to become more focused on the development of the people who are working under your supervision?

9. What did you learn from this chapter and how can you apply it?

10. What areas do you need to pray about or improve in?

Great Supportive Ministers Are People of Integrity and Honesty

But you desire honesty from the heart....

—Psalm 51:6 (*NLT*)

Lying lips are an abomination to the Lord, but those who deal truthfully are His delight.

—Proverbs 12:22

I once conducted a survey among senior pastors and asked them which traits they valued most among their staff and key leaders. I wasn't surprised that *loyalty* was the most commonly cited characteristic—I expected that. However, I was surprised that *honesty* came in second. I had taken honesty for granted, believing that every supportive minister (and Christian for that matter!) would of course be honest. Nevertheless, this issue was on the forefront of many pastors' minds.

When I began to think through this honesty issue in the light of God's Word, I realized there were several examples of biblical characters—even high-profile ones—who did not always operate in honesty:

- Abraham told both Pharaoh and Abimilech that Sarah (his wife) was his sister (Gen. 12:13; 20:2).

- After Aaron took an engraving tool and carved the golden calf, he misrepresented the facts when he told Moses that he had simply put the gold in the fire and "out came this calf" (Exod. 32:24 *NLT*).
- Gehazi got greedy when Elisha declined the gifts offered by Naaman (2 Kings 5:20–27). So Gehazi pursued Naaman, misrepresented his master Elisha, lied to Naaman, and took gold and clothing from Naaman under false pretenses. To top off all his dishonest behavior, Gehazi then lied to Elisha about the whole thing! The *Message* says, "He [Gehazi] returned and stood before his master. Elisha said, 'So what have you been up to, Gehazi?' 'Nothing much,' he said" (2 Kings 5:25).

Whether or not you deal honestly in life is determined by your character. If you want to be a person of integrity, you must practice honesty.

Samuel in the Old Testament set an example for us to follow if we want to be people of honesty and integrity. In his farewell address, Samuel invited the people to identify any fraud, dishonesty, or exploitative behavior he had engaged in during his lifetime. Samuel's conscience was clear, because he knew he had conducted his ministry in a manner that was above reproach—he had lived his life as a man of integrity. Here is what he said in First Samuel chapter 12.

1 SAMUEL 12:2–5 (*NLT*)

2   ...I stand here, an old, gray-haired man. I have served as your leader since I was a boy.

3   Now tell me as I stand before the Lord and before his anointed one—whose ox or donkey have I stolen? Have I ever cheated any of you? Have I ever oppressed you? Have I ever taken a bribe? Tell me and I will make right whatever I have done wrong."

4   "No," they replied, "you have never cheated or oppressed us in any way, and you have never taken even a single bribe."

5 "The Lord and his anointed one are my witnesses,"
   Samuel declared, "that you can never accuse me of
   robbing you." "Yes, it is true," they replied.

If you are always honest and full of integrity, you will have
the same testimony Samuel had. At the end of your ministry,
you can ask, "Have I ever cheated anyone? Have I ever
oppressed anyone?" and the answer will be, "No, you have
been honest throughout your life and have lived your life
above reproach."

Paul Set the Example for Us

Living in integrity and above reproach was also very
important to the Apostle Paul. When you consider the qualifi-
cations he gave for key church leaders in First Timothy 3:1–13
and Titus 1:6–9, you will note that most of the qualifying
issues have to do with character and moral uprightness—not
with technical skills or ministerial expertise. Paul wanted those
ministering in the Church to have high standards of integrity,
to be respectable individuals, and to be people whose lives
would be a good example of what Christianity was all about.

Paul didn't merely set high standards for others; he embraced
and embodied them himself. Paul avoided wrong-doing in every
area of life, but he also took his moral integrity and high character a step farther—he made sure his behavior never gave
grounds for even the *suspicion* of wrong behavior.

When Paul was carrying an offering from various churches
designated for the poor in Jerusalem, he said, "We want to
avoid any criticism of the way we administer this liberal gift.
For we are taking pains to do what is right, not only in the eyes
of the Lord but also in the eyes of men" (2 Cor. 8:20–21 *NIV*).
In the *Message* version of this passage, Paul referred to "taking
every precaution against scandal," and then said, "We don't
want anyone suspecting us of taking one penny of this money
for ourselves. We're being as careful in our reputation with the
public as in our reputation with God" (2 Cor. 8:20–21).

No 'Double Tongues' Allowed!

One of the requirements for those chosen to assist the apostles in daily distribution to the widows was that they be "men of honest report" (Acts 6:3). Paul said these deacons (those who serve in the church) must not be "double-tongued" (1 Tim. 3:8). The Greek word translated "double-tongued" is "dilogos," which is from two different Greek words. The first Greek word means *twice* and the other Greek word ("logos") means *something said.*[1] In the context of First Timothy 3:8, Paul is referring to a person who says two different things about the same subject.

The *Amplified Bible* translates the first part of First Timothy 3:8 this way: "The deacons [must be] worthy of respect, not shifty and *double-talkers but sincere in what they say.*" Today, the word "two-faced" is sometimes used to describe a person who says two different things about the same subject or who acts one way in front of certain people and an entirely different way in front of others. Paul admonished pastors to choose supportive ministers who were neither hypocritical nor dishonest.

There Are No 'Little White Lies'

Some people differentiate between "big lies" and "little lies," and we somehow think that little lies are acceptable. A person told me once that he had called a church office and asked to speak to a minister. The person calling then heard a muffled conversation between the secretary and the minister. He heard the minister say in the background, "Tell him I'm not here." What do you think that dishonest action did to that pastor's reputation? How do you think it made the caller feel?

Some people might consider what the pastor did to be a "little white lie," but dishonesty damages one's credibility and trustworthiness. Dishonesty—any amount of dishonesty—breeds distrust. After all, if a person is willing to lie in one situation, what would stop him from lying in another?

People of good character (integrity) have the following attributes:

- They are above board, honorable, and pure in all their dealings.
- They are not deceitful. They don't do things in secret that they would be ashamed of in the light.
- They tell the truth. If they are wrong or make a mistake, they admit it—they accept responsibility for their actions. They don't blame-shift, spin, slant, or twist the story to their own advantage.
- They don't say things which are technically true in one sense, but actually give a false impression of the overall situation.
- They are accurate in stating the facts. They don't embellish or exaggerate, and they don't withhold pertinent and appropriate information.
- They keep their word. They do what they say they are going to do. They don't make rash, impulsive promises that they can't or don't intend to keep.
- They say "yes" when they mean yes, and they say "no" when they mean no.

These attributes should be characteristic of every supportive minister in every area of life. When we are honest with people in our everyday dealings, they will be more likely to believe us when we tell them about Jesus.

When I think of honesty, I am reminded that nearly all parents have told their children, "Whatever happens, I want you tell me the truth. If you make a mistake or do something wrong and honestly admit it, I'll forgive you and work with you—just don't lie to me about it." Pastors feel the same way about their "family" of staff members. They want to know that their supportive ministers will be honest with them. Trust is the basis of working together, and consistent honesty is the basis of trust.

QUESTIONS FOR REFLECTION AND DISCUSSION

1. When you study the situations discussed in this chapter involving Abraham, Aaron, and Gehazi, it is obvious that

they attempted to suppress the truth. Have you ever done something similar in order to suppress the full truth?

2. Have you made a heartfelt decision to be completely honest even when you may feel pressure to bend or hide part of the truth?
3. Have you made a commitment to finish your ministry with the same kind of testimony that Samuel had?
4. In addition to avoiding wrongdoing in every area, do you also avoid conduct that could imply wrongdoing?
5. Are there any actions that could give people grounds for falsely doubting your character? How can you change these actions to eliminate possible suspicion?
6. If you make a mistake or are wrong about something, do you readily admit it and accept responsibility, or are you tempted to blame-shift, minimize, or twist the story to cover your tracks?
7. Have you ever been tempted to embellish or exaggerate in relating an incident?
8. Do you keep your word? Does your "yes" mean yes and your "no" mean no?
9. What did you learn from this chapter and how can you apply it?
10. What areas do you need to pray about or improve in?

---

[1] James Strong, "Greek Dictionary of the New Testament," *The New Strong's Exhaustive Concordance of the Bible* (Nashville: Thomas Nelson, 1984), 23.

Great Supportive Ministers Exercise Wisdom in Their Pulpit Ministry

Not all who work in supportive ministry will be preachers or teachers. In First Peter 4:11, Peter referred to those who minister to the Body of Christ by *speaking* and also to those who minister by *serving*. People who work behind the pulpit and those who work behind the scenes both make a valuable contribution to the Church.

Some senior pastors are understandably leery about allowing others to preach in their pulpit because they've seen people exploit the opportunity for their own personal advancement instead of seeking the benefit and unity of the church overall. A pastor needs people he can trust who will genuinely seek to build up the church, not people who will abuse the opportunity to preach and use it for self-gain or to undermine him.

If you do have speaking responsibilities as a supportive minister (whether it is to the congregation as a whole or to a smaller class or group), there are some important guidelines to remember. Following these guidelines will increase your value to the pastor and prove your ability to act in wise, responsible ways when entrusted with pulpit duties.

Don't Give Direction
or Correction

As a general rule, both *direction* and *correction* for the church body should come from the senior pastor, not from someone in supportive ministry. If you are a department head or a supervisor, you may be expected to direct ministry and correct specific problems within your particular area of oversight—but even this is to be done with respect to the overall vision and values of the church.

The role of a supportive minister in the pulpit is generally to support and reinforce basic truths of Scripture and to provide instruction that is edifying in nature. Of course, some scriptures are intrinsically corrective in nature, and I'm not saying you must entirely avoid those, but don't make it your mission to straighten out everything that you think is wrong in the church.

Avoid Controversial Subjects

When asked to preach, supportive ministers should also avoid highly controversial subjects that tend to create confusion or division. The pastor does not want to have to clean up the "messes" created by other speakers. If you have a question about whether or not a topic is appropriate, ask the pastor *before* you speak.

Never put the pastor on the spot by publicly saying something like, "Pastor, God is leading me to say something that might be controversial. Is it okay if I obey God?" What is the pastor supposed to say at that point? Is he supposed to tell you that you're not to obey God? Don't put the pastor in that kind of position.

Be clear on such issues well in advance of your speaking date, and don't get offended if the pastor asks you not to teach on certain subjects or to refrain from addressing certain issues. Keep in mind that God wants you to respect authority. God wants you to honor the pastor's wishes, so He will never lead you to preach something from the pulpit or force you to say something that is in direct opposition to what your pastor has asked of you (see 1 Corinthians 14:32–33).

Don't Be Flashy

Supportive ministers should not try to outdo the pastor or to razzle-dazzle the people with their preaching skills. Avoid unnecessary flamboyance. You are not on staff to garner popularity or to create a following for yourself—you are there to supplement the rest of the ministry that is taking place. Use any pulpit opportunities you might receive to bless, not to impress.

Receive Compliments With a Grain of Salt

Also, don't let it go to your head if someone tells you he prefers your preaching to that of the senior pastor. There will always be people who prefer one style over another. That doesn't mean you're more anointed or a better preacher than the pastor, and it doesn't mean you're supposed to take his place. Keep in mind that as a supportive minister, you are probably preaching less frequently than the senior pastor, which means there is a familiarity factor that comes into play. People tend to devalue what they are most accustomed to and rave about something that is new and different. If the roles were reversed, and the people heard you more frequently, they might also find it refreshing when they heard someone other than you!

Don't Rearrange the Furniture

It is also important to make sure that what you are teaching is consistent with the beliefs, doctrines, and vision of the church and pastor. You wouldn't go into someone's home and rearrange their furniture; you wouldn't go into a farmer's field and plow it cross-grained. You ought to treat the church with the same respect—it's not your church. That means you don't get up and knowingly preach a message that contradicts something your pastor has taught.

You and your pastor may not agree on everything. However, if you are a leader in your church, then you should agree with your pastor on the essential issues of the

> YOU ARE NOT ON STAFF TO GARNER POPULARITY OR TO CREATE A FOLLOWING FOR YOURSELF—YOU ARE THERE TO SUPPLEMENT THE REST OF THE MINISTRY THAT IS TAKING PLACE.

Bible. You may perhaps see things differently when it comes to some of the minor, less significant parts of Scripture. Learn to major on the majors, and if you disagree on some minor points, leave them alone and keep your opinions to yourself. Preach from common ground—things on which you and the pastor do see eye-to-eye.

Some people seem to have an obsession with quibbling over doctrines that don't make any difference one way or another. They become dogmatic over nonessentials and end up causing confusion and division over petty issues. Some people seem driven to come up with some newfangled doctrine that no one has ever thought of before. Both of these tendencies (splitting hairs and trying to be inventive with Scripture) will get you into trouble—in the pulpit and out of it.

Consider some of Paul's admonitions to Timothy along these lines:

1 TIMOTHY 1:3–6

3   … Charge some that they teach no other doctrine,

4   nor give heed to fables and endless genealogies, which cause disputes rather than godly edification which is in faith.

5   Now the purpose of the commandment is love from a pure heart, from a good conscience, and from sincere faith,

6   from which some, having strayed, have turned aside to
    idle talk.

2 TIMOTHY 1:13

13 Hold fast the pattern of sound words which you have
    heard from me, in faith and love which are in Christ
    Jesus.

2 TIMOTHY 2:14–16

14 Remind them of these things, charging them before the
    Lord not to strive about words to no profit, to the ruin
    of the hearers.

15 Be diligent to present yourself approved to God, a
    worker who does not need to be ashamed, rightly
    dividing the word of truth.

16 But shun profane and idle babblings, for they will
    increase to more ungodliness.

2 TIMOTHY 4:3–4 (*NLT*)

3   For a time is coming when people will no longer listen
    to right teaching. They will follow their own desires
    and will look for teachers who will tell them whatever
    they want to hear.

4   They will reject the truth and follow strange myths.

Paul is essentially telling Timothy to stay with the basics
and not to get caught up in pursuing weird and unprofitable
tangents. Learn to interpret the Bible well and to teach it in a
way that truly edifies and helps people. If you do these things,
your time in the pulpit will be a blessing to the church and to
the pastor.

If your goal and ultimate calling is to have a pulpit ministry, take care of your pastor's pulpit. Luke 16:12 says, *"If you
have not been faithful in what is another man's, who will give you
what is your own?"* As a supportive minister, exercise wisdom
and prove yourself to be responsible and opportunities to
preach will most likely increase. If you prove yourself to be

unwise and irresponsible, don't be surprised if the pulpit rightly remains off limits.

QUESTIONS FOR REFLECTION AND DISCUSSION

1. In light of your particular supportive ministry responsibilities, how does the guideline "direction and correction for the church at-large should come from the senior pastor" impact your duties?
2. Are you keeping your pulpit ministry basic? Are you supplementing and reinforcing what the pastor is already teaching?
3. Are you avoiding controversial subjects in your teachings? Are you avoiding issues that might cause confusion and division among the people?
4. Is your teaching consistent with the beliefs, doctrines, and vision of your church and pastor?
5. What are the majors that you major on?
6. If the pastor asked you not to teach on a certain topic, would you be respectful of that request and abide by it?
7. What did you learn from this chapter and how can you apply it?
8. What areas do you need to pray about or improve in?

Great Supportive Ministers Demonstrate Discretion

Genesis 41:33 says, "Now therefore let Pharaoh look out a man *discreet* and wise, and set him over the land of Egypt" (*KJV*). In the Hebrew language, this word "discreet" means *to understand, deal wisely, consider, pay attention to, regard, notice, discern, perceive, inquire.*[1] It also means *to separate mentally* or *distinguish* or *to understand.*[2]

When we say someone has discretion, we typically mean he is intelligent and has a keen sense of the right things to say and do in any given situation. A discreet person avoids saying the wrong things at the wrong time to the wrong people, and also avoids taking inappropriate action (or taking proper action but at the wrong time or in the wrong setting). A discreet person has good judgment—sensitivity to what is fitting and appropriate—and behaves accordingly.

The Apostle Paul wanted his young associate Timothy to know how to carry himself in ministry. Paul told him, *"I write so that you may know how you ought to conduct yourself in the house of God, which is the church of the living God"* (1 Tim. 3:15). As supportive ministers we must also know how to carry ourselves in ministry and how to conduct ourselves in the house of God.

Paul taught that when bondservants acted properly, they were *"showing all good fidelity,"* and, as a result, they *"adorn the doctrine of God our Savior in all things"* (Titus 2:9–10). The *New Living Translation* renders this passage, "…They must show themselves to be entirely trustworthy and good. Then they will make the teaching about God our Savior attractive in every way."

As servants of God, our conduct should always enhance, not hinder, the spread of the Gospel. If right conduct can make the Gospel attractive, then wrong conduct can make the Gospel unattractive. If we are rude, behave unmannerly and tackily, or do things that are in bad taste, then our effectiveness in working for God greatly diminishes. Instead of behaving graciously, some supportive ministers are more like the proverbial bull in a china shop, constantly bringing unnecessary offense to others.

> IF RIGHT CONDUCT CAN MAKE THE GOSPEL ATTRACTIVE, THEN WRONG CONDUCT CAN MAKE THE GOSPEL UNATTRACTIVE.

Secular companies realize that it is good for business when their employees provide good customer service, are efficient, and treat people with kindness and courtesy. How much more should Christian organizations provide service that is excellent in every way? Unfortunately, "the children of this world are in their generation wiser than the children of light" (Luke 16:8 *KJV*). At times, the Church has lagged behind various secular organizations in terms of establishing and maintaining excellence when it comes to connecting with and serving its target audience.

What Discretion Looks Like

Psalm 112:5 says that a good man *"…will guide his affairs with discretion."* What are some traits of people who have discretion?
- Their words and actions are not in poor taste.
- They carry themselves with a proper sense of dignity and respectability.

- They conduct themselves with an appropriate level of professionalism in their work and in their dealings with others.
- They respect the boundaries of others, not intruding inappropriately into another person's "private space."
- They demonstrate proper decorum, exhibiting politeness, courtesy, and good manners.
- They understand and follow the chain of command; they honor proper protocol in their conduct and communications.
- They are a class act.
- Their physical appearance, hygiene, and grooming is appropriate, and they are modest in their dress.
- They show good judgment in handling difficult situations.

Based on this list of traits, how discreet have you been in your supportive ministry? Is there any room for improvement?

Discretion Means
Keeping Confidentiality

A major part of discretion is the ability to maintain confidentiality and to properly handle sensitive information. Various positions in a church may allow you access to information that is not appropriate to share with others. For example, if you are trusted to count the offering, you should not discuss with others how much money people gave.

If you are a minister who counsels church members, you should not reveal to other people what someone tells you in a counseling session. In fact, you should not reveal even the basic fact that So-and-so has been to the church for counseling. That is a breech of confidentiality. If people go to see a minister to discuss a personal issue, they don't expect their visit to be broadcast to others—they expect their privacy to be respected, *and it should be.*

Don't be a gossip or a busybody. The Apostle Paul warned a church that some of them were "wasting time meddling in other people's business" (2 Thess. 3:11 *NLT*). The *New Testament in Basic English* renders Paul's description of busybodies in First Timothy 5:13 as "being over interested in the business of others." Staff members and church leaders should be careful to not allow their care and concern for the people to lead to gossip or nosiness–being "over interested" in the business of others.

Some people feel important when they reveal "inside information," but the very fact that they would inappropriately reveal and discuss such information only demonstrates that they are not qualified for positions of responsibility. Supportive ministers must recognize the trust that has been extended toward them, and honor that trust by being faithful, responsible, and mature.

Discretion Means Keeping Your Cool

Proverbs 19:11 says, *"The discretion of a man makes him slow to anger, And his glory is to overlook a transgression."* A person of discretion is not going to overreact to every imperfection he notices; he knows it's not his job to correct every minute flaw in people or an organization.

Solomon noted how unpleasant it is when a person lacks discretion. He said, *"As a ring of gold in a swine's snout, So is a lovely woman who lacks discretion"* (Prov. 11:22). What a picture this verse paints! Solomon's comparison can also apply to a person who holds a position of trust in the church, but lacks discretion, tact, and professionalism. Some people may appear to be talented and have a respectable position, but if they don't have the wisdom to act and speak with discretion, whatever seemed respectable will soon be overshadowed by their lack of good taste and dignity.

William Shakespeare famously wrote, "Discretion is the better part of valor." In other words, it is better to be cautious than to act rashly. If you ever wonder what action to take as a supportive minister, err on the side of caution. When in doubt, choose discretion and you and the church will reap the benefits.

QUESTIONS FOR REFLECTION AND DISCUSSION

1. Does your conduct enhance or hinder the health of the church and the spread of the Gospel?
2. Does your behavior draw people to the Gospel or repel them?
3. How do you "make the teaching about God our Savior attractive in every way"?
4. In what ways do you help the church provide excellent, high-caliber service?
5. Do you conduct yourself with dignity, respect, and with an appropriate level of professionalism in your work for God?
6. Are you polite and courteous, exhibiting good manners?
7. Do you maintain good hygiene and grooming? Are you modest and appropriate in the way you dress and present yourself?
8. Do you avoid gossip?
9. Do you keep confidential information confidential?
10. Do you exhibit discretion in the sense that you don't feel obligated to make note of and correct every imperfection you see?
11. What did you learn from this chapter and how can you apply it?
12. What areas do you need to pray about or improve in?

---

[1] W.E. Vine, Merrill F. Unger, and William White Jr., "Old Testament Section," *Vine's Expository Dictionary of Biblical Words* (Nashville: Thomas Nelson, 1985), 273.

[2] James Strong, "Hebrew and Chaldee Dictionary," *The New Strong's Exhaustive Concordance of the Bible* (Nashville: Thomas Nelson, 1984), 20.

PART IV

Staying Free From Staff Infection

In the previous section, we examined some of the character traits that great supportive ministers embody and exemplify. Some of these characteristics included loyalty, faithfulness, balance, flexibility, internal motivation, honesty, and wisdom. The traits examined in Part III of this book are not meant to be an exhaustive list, but are to provide a strong foundation upon which you can build additional qualities and habits.

Now that you know what attributes supportive ministers should embrace, let's study what supportive ministers should avoid like the plague—*staff infection*. In the next few chapters, we will define staff infection and discover how to avoid it. We will also look at biblical examples of those who suffered from this condition and the destruction it caused in their life and ministry.

Avoiding
Staff Infection

Naturally speaking, an infection in the body results when a bacteria or virus grows in an area it should not be and grows in a way that overcomes the body's natural defenses. There are natural things we can do to help us maintain physical health: eat a good diet, obtain adequate rest, engage in ample exercise, properly manage stress, and so forth. One of the ways these disciplines promote good physical health is that they help keep our immune system strong. A strong immune system enables our body to fight off infections that would try to harm us. If our immune system is weakened or deficient, then our body is more likely to get sick.

I believe there are many correlations between an infection in the physical body and "infections" that can take place in the Body of Christ. There are various "bacteria" that can weaken our spiritual immune system, so to speak, and hinder our ability to fight "staff infection." There are also various disciplines staff members can employ to keep the "immune system" strong and to prevent infection from taking hold.

Supportive ministers typically begin their work in the church with joy and enthusiasm, but often find themselves fighting to maintain a good attitude and a positive outlook. At times, an entire staff or group of workers can be affected, causing overall morale to greatly suffer. Left untreated, these frustrations can weaken and cripple the ministry within the church.

It is possible for a church staff to stay healthy

> IT IS POSSIBLE FOR A CHURCH STAFF TO STAY HEALTHY AND VIBRANT, BUT ONLY IF THE MEMBERS BUILD UP RESISTANCE TO THE COMMON DISEASES THAT AFFECT CHURCH STAFFS AND LEADERSHIP TEAMS.

and vibrant, but only if the members build up resistance to the common diseases that affect church staffs and leadership teams. Let's identify and study some of the factors that weaken our spiritual immune system and make us vulnerable to staff infection.

Don't Let Irritation Lead to Infection

Dealing with difficult people is one of the most taxing and challenging things any minister will face. Bible commentator Harry Ironside made a simple, yet profound statement: "Wherever there's light, there's bugs."[1] These "bugs," or difficult people, make it a challenge to remain constantly hopeful and optimistic in ministry. While it may be a challenge to deal with difficult people and still remain vibrant, it isn't impossible. It just requires more of God's grace!

I was talking to one pastor who mentioned his dealings with some of his "EGR Members." Try as I might, I could not figure out what he meant by that term. When I asked him about it, he responded, "Those are my "Extra-Grace-Required Members." Do you work with people whom you could term EGR Members? Don't worry; God has the extra grace required!

We are always going to have a challenge of one sort or another. As author G. Douglass Lewis said, "The option for human beings, however, is not whether to experience conflict or not. The only choice is whether this conflict will be managed constructively or destructively."[2] Great supportive ministers choose to manage conflict constructively.

Noted pastor and author Rick Warren once commented, "Every small group has at least one 'difficult' person in it. If you don't immediately recognize who that person is—it's probably you!" [3] While we surely don't want to get "staff infection" caused by the prolonged frustrations of dealing with difficult people, let's also make especially sure that *we* are never the difficult people who are challenging the joy and peace of others!

Early in ministry, I realized how many problems, challenges, and difficulties the pastor has to deal within leading a church. Most noticeable was the challenge of dealing with difficult people. While the majority of the people in a church are wonderful and supportive, some can be highly unsupportive. Different people express their non-support in different ways:

- Some are opinionated critics and complainers.
- Others register their disapproval by becoming passive-aggressive.
- Some want (and demand that) everything be done their way.
- Some are negative and pessimistic, spreading their discontent to others.
- Some will make commitments and not follow through.
- Others may gossip and say things behind the pastor's back (even though they might act very respectful to his face).

Observing these "problem people" and recognizing the negative impact of their actions, I prayed, "Lord, may I never be a problem or a source of frustration for the pastor. I ask You to help me to always be an asset to him and never one of his problems." I encourage you to make that your prayer as well and to reflect for a moment upon whether or not your actions lend support to the pastor or add to his list of problems. Do any of the traits and actions in the bulleted list describe your behavior? If so, it's time for a change. Make the commitment to support your pastor and to eliminate any trace of infection from your ministry service.

The Three Fs:
Fatigue, Flattery, and Frustration

Dealing with difficult people is one factor that can weaken our spiritual immune system. Another factor that can lower our resistance to staff infection is *fatigue*, so we must guard against it in our work for God. Whether it's physical, mental, emotional, or spiritual fatigue, we need to guard against becoming "weary in well doing" (Gal. 6:9). Becoming weary tends to lead to becoming irritable. As we grow weary, our tolerance for the shortcomings of others starts to diminish. The fact that fatigue can cause us to act in ways we normally would not does not give us a license to act ugly "just because we're tired." Rather, knowing these physiological facts should inspire us to guard against fatigue and to strive to serve in the most productive, healthy way possible.

A second factor that can weaken our immune system and make us more susceptible to staff infection is *flattery*. There's nothing wrong with a sincere word of appreciation or encouragement—that's not what we mean when we use the word "flattery." Encarta Dictionary defines "flattery" as *an act or instance of complimenting somebody, often excessively or insincerely, especially in order to get something.*[4]

Supportive ministers must be very careful when people flatter them. Here is one example of such flattery: A church member approaches the associate pastor after a service and says, "I like your preaching better than the senior pastor's. You feed me more than he does." Wait a minute! This is not a talent contest! Remember, the associate pastor (and every other supportive minister) is there to help and assist the pastor—not to compete with him or to outdo him.

Here's another scenario: After you sing a solo or lead a worship song people tell you, "You sure did a great job. I don't know why they don't let you sing more often." Again, there's nothing wrong with a basic compliment, but what happens when the singer starts thinking, *Yeah, why DON'T they let me sing more often? I'm better than all those other people.* The next thing you know, there is envy, jealousy, resentment, self-promotion, and numerous other infectious elements festering within you. It's only a matter of time before that infection starts to spread to other people in the church.

The third "F" that can lower our immunity to staff infection is *frustration*. It's great to have high aspirations and standards, but sometimes we become unrealistic and perfectionistic in our expectations which leads to disappointment and frustration. In fact, the amount of difference between our expectations and our reality determines the amount of disappointment and frustration we feel. The greater the difference between what we expect to happen and what actually happens, the greater the amount of disappointment and frustration.

Prolonged frustration also leads to staff infection and causes people to experience negative symptoms. People suffering from this kind of staff infection become critical and fault-finding. To defend against this, we need to remember that it's not our job to make the church perfect, and it's not healthy to expect it to be so. As long as there are human beings involved in the church (which includes you too), there will not be flawless perfection. I like what Max Lucado said, "...be realistic. Lower your expectations of earth. This is not heaven, so don't expect it to be." [5]

Rick Warren was addressing having realistic expectations when he said the following:

> It is easy to become discouraged by the gap between the *ideal* and the *real* in your church. Yet we must passionately love the church in spite of its imperfections. Longing for the ideal while criticizing the real is evidence of immaturity. On the other hand, settling for the real without striving for the ideal is complacency. Maturity is living with the tension. [6]

If you have a legitimate frustration, deal with it in a mature and constructive way. *Pray.* Keep in mind that you're not necessarily going to agree with every single decision that is made, and you're not going to feel that everything in the church is done perfectly. You can, however, still keep a good attitude. Choose to focus on the good and the positive, and keep moving forward for the good of the team.

Disagree Without Being Disagreeable

In speaking to pastors about selecting leaders, Rick Renner said the following about how people handle disagreement:

Disagreement is just a part of life. So no matter how peaceable and kind a potential leader seems right now, just expect it to happen at some point in the future.

Given the inevitability of disagreement, it's far better to find out how the potential leader handles conflict and disagreement *before* you've established him in a highly visible position of leadership. If you discover this person can't handle conflict, it's better not to use him as a leader. If he doesn't have the maturity to disagree and walk in unity at the same time, he isn't mature enough yet to stand in a position of leadership.[7]

Frustrations can exist in relationships that have numerous good qualities, but if people are focused on the problems and consumed with only what's wrong, they fail to see the overall good that is present. They are then wide open to catching a bad case of staff infection, or, even worse, causing a widespread outbreak.

As you stand guard against staff infection, focus on keeping your spiritual immune system strong. Watch out for irritation, fatigue, flattery, and frustration; and learn to disagree without being disagreeable. As Kevin E. Lawson wrote, "The ability to thrive is based not on the absence of stress or frustrating situations but on the ability to work in the midst of them, not growing excessively discouraged or drained by them." [8] Keep your immune system strong, and the inevitable stresses of ministry won't lead to staff infection!

QUESTIONS FOR REFLECTION AND DISCUSSION

1. How is your spiritual immune system? Are you built up in resisting staff infection?
2. How are you doing in the area of fatigue? Do you get enough sleep? Do you give your physical body adequate time to rest and recover?
3. What do you do to stay spiritually and emotionally refreshed in the Lord?
4. Have you ever grown weary in well-doing? What did you do to get your strength back?
5. Do you guard against letting flattery going to your head?
6. Have you ever let someone's compliment pit you against the pastor or another leader? What was the result?
7. How do you handle frustration?
8. Would you say you have realistic or unrealistic expectations?
9. What can you do to remind yourself to stay focused on the positive?
10. What did you learn from this chapter and how can you apply it?
11. What areas do you need to pray about or improve in?

---

[1] Marhall Shelley, *Well-Intentioned Dragons* (Carol Stream, IL: Word Books, 1985), 12.

[2] Stand-alone quote from *Resolving Church Conflicts* by G. Douglass Lewis. Copyright © 1981 by G. Douglass Lewis. Reprinted by permission of HarperCollins Publishers.

[3] Rick Warren, "Saddleback Sayings," *Rick Warren's Ministry Toolbox*, Issue 1, March 19, 2001, http://www.pastors.com/RWMT/?ID=1.

[4] *Encarta Dictionary Online*, s.v. "Flattery," http://encarta.msn.com/dictionary_ /flattery.html.

[5] Max Lucado, *When God Whispers Your Name* (Nashville: W Publishing Group, 1999), 169.

[6] Taken from *Purpose-Driven® Life, The* by Rick Warren. Copyright © 2002 by Rick Warren. Used by permission of The Zondervan Corporation.

[7] Rick Renner, *Who Is Ready for a Spiritual Promotion?* (Tulsa: Teach All Nations, 2000), 223. Used by permission.

[8] Reprinted from *How to Thrive in Associate Staff Ministry* by Kevin E. Lawson, with permission from the Alban Institute. Copyright © 2000 by The Alban Institute, Inc. All rights reserved.

Under the Influence

Staff infection can assail even the best of staffs—Jesus' staff of disciples being the prime example. When it comes to bad staff members in the Bible, perhaps no one comes to mind so quickly as Judas Iscariot. Satan used Judas' proximity to Jesus and influenced him to betray Jesus.

It's interesting that the betrayal was expressed through a kiss—a common expression of affection in that culture. This situation illustrates a very painful truth, that those who are closest to a leader have the greatest potential of hurting him. The pain of this type of betrayal is dynamically expressed in Psalm chapter 55:

PSALM 55:12-14,21

12   For it is not an enemy who reproaches me; Then I could bear it. Nor is it one who hates me who has exalted himself against me; Then I could hide from him.

13   But it was you, a man my equal, My companion and my acquaintance.

14   We took sweet counsel together, And walked to the house of God in the throng....

21   The words of his mouth were smoother than butter, But war was in his heart; His words were softer than oil, Yet they were drawn swords.

As supportive ministers, we need to be careful to never misuse our proximity to a spiritual leader or to violate the trust that has been given to us. That proximity and trust is ours because we are expected to help that person. To feign affection and loyalty while undermining a leader is the epitome of betrayal, and that's why the pain expressed in Psalm chapter 55 is so intense.

While it is easy to single out Judas as a cause of infection on Jesus' staff, there were other disciples who also caused infection and presented challenges to Jesus. I doubt Peter, James, or John ever got up in the morning and said, "You know, I think I'd like to really make life difficult for Jesus today. Instead of conforming to His plan and helping Him fulfill His destiny, I'd like to be a real hindrance." And yet these three disciples *were* a hindrance from time to time. I don't think the problems they caused were deliberate, but they happened nonetheless, proving that staff infection can happen to any of us!

> THERE WAS A PROBLEM OF COMPARISON AND COMPETITIVENESS THAT EXISTED AMONG JESUS' STAFF, AND IF WE ALLOW HUMAN NATURE TO DICTATE OUR ACTIONS, THERE WILL BE QUARRELS AMONG US TOO!

In this chapter, we will study these occurrences of staff infection among Jesus' disciples and discover that infection can be caused by yielding to and operating under the wrong influence. Although the disciples generally yielded to the right influence, there were times when they yielded to a wrong spiritual influence. Other times, the disciples simply allowed their carnal nature or human personality to dictate their actions.

Yielding to the Carnal Nature

On at least three occasions, Jesus' disciples argued about which of them was the greatest. One of these heated discussions even took place at the Last Supper (Luke 22:24–27)! There was a problem of comparison and competitiveness that existed among Jesus' staff, and if we allow human nature to dictate our actions, there will be quarrels among us too! It's human nature to focus on others, but we need to focus on obeying what God has called us to do.

We've seen throughout *In Search of Timothy* that we're not to compete with the pastor. Likewise, we're not to compete with our fellow supportive members—whether it's to gain favor with the people or with the pastor. Our motivation must not be about who is going to be the greatest, or who will receive the most recognition, but about how we can work together as a team to serve others.

Peter learned this principle in John chapter 21.

JOHN 21:17,19–22

17 [Jesus] **said to** [Peter] **the third time, "Simon, son of Jonah, do you love Me?" Peter was grieved because He said to him the third time, "Do you love Me?" And he said to Him, "Lord, You know all things; You know that I love You." Jesus said to him, "Feed My sheep"....**

19 **...And when He had spoken this, He said to him, "Follow Me."**

20 **Then Peter, turning around, saw the disciple whom Jesus loved following, who also had leaned on His breast at the supper, and said, "Lord, who is the one who betrays You?"**

21 **Peter, seeing him, said to Jesus, "But Lord, what about this man?"**

22 **Jesus said to him, "If I will that he remain till I come, what is that to you? You follow Me."**

Up until that time, Peter had been concerned with John's role in the Kingdom. When Peter asked, "Lord, what about this man?" it was that old issue of comparison and competition resurfacing. But when Jesus told him, "Feed my sheep" it was all about *compassion* for others. Peter had to learn to take his eyes off of John and to simply follow Jesus.

Yielding to the Devil's Influence

Peter had other moments when he yielded to the wrong influence. In John chapter 21, Peter yielded to his carnal, competitive nature. But in Matthew chapter 16, Peter inadvertently yielded to

> EVEN STALWART BELIEVERS CAN GO FROM WALKING IN THE SPIRIT TO YIELDING TO THE WRONG INFLUENCE IN A SHORT AMOUNT OF TIME.

the *devil's* influence. Peter often responded to the right influence, but this passage in Matthew teaches us that even stalwart believers can go from walking in the Spirit to yielding to the wrong influence in a short amount of time.

MATTHEW 16:15–18
15　He said to them, "But who do you say that I am?"
16　Simon Peter answered and said, "You are the Christ, the Son of the living God."
17　Jesus answered and said to him, "Blessed are you, Simon Bar-Jonah, for flesh and blood has not revealed this to you, but My Father who is in heaven.
18　And I also say to you that you are Peter, and on this rock I will build My church, and the gates of Hades shall not prevail against it."

One of the highlights in Peter's walk with the Lord occurred when he received this spiritual insight–revelation knowledge from God about the true identity of Jesus. That bright spot in Peter's life dimmed quickly. After receiving insight from the right Source, Peter inadvertently yielded to the wrong source. Consider the sharp contrast between Peter's conversation with Jesus in the previous passage and their conversation in the following encounter:

MATTHEW 16:21–23
21　From that time Jesus began to show to His disciples that He must go to Jerusalem, and suffer many things

**from the elders and chief priests and scribes, and be
killed, and be raised the third day.**

22 **Then Peter took Him aside and began to rebuke Him,
saying, "Far be it from You, Lord; this shall not happen
to You!"**

23 **But He turned and said to Peter, "Get behind Me,
Satan! You are an offense to Me, for you are not mindful of the things of God, but the things of men."**

In verse 17 it's, *"Blessed are you, Simon Bar-Jonah."* In verse
23 it's, *"Get behind Me, Satan."* How can a person go from
receiving spiritual illumination from God in one instance to
being deceived by Satan shortly thereafter? That's quite a
shift—a quick on-set of staff infection!

We see that Peter yielded to the carnal nature, which
caused him to struggle with competition and comparison—two
forms of staff infection. Peter also yielded to the devil and
allowed a different form of staff infection to seep into his relationship with Jesus. (Thankfully, Jesus did not succumb to the
infection, or we wouldn't be saved today!)

James and John:
The Sons of Thunder

James and John also experienced and expressed conflicting
influences. Like Peter, they yielded to a wrong spiritual influence in one instance. In other situations, they simply walked
in carnality and allowed staff infection to set in.

Mark 3:17 tells us that Jesus nicknamed James and John
the "Sons of Thunder." This was probably because they were
loud and boisterous and had a tendency to stir things up a bit.
Now we refer to John as the "Apostle of Love" and rightly so,
but John wasn't always known for being loving and gentle.

Right after Jesus taught the disciples about becoming as little
children, John told Jesus, *"Teacher, we saw someone who does not*

follow us casting out demons in Your name, and we forbade him because he does not follow us" (Mark 9:38). Jesus had to correct John for having an attitude of exclusivity and superiority concerning ministry.

We already know that the disciples had significant strife and numerous arguments about which of them was the greatest. One of these arguments was sparked when John and James went to Jesus privately and requested the seats of highest honor in His Kingdom (Mark 10:35–45).

People with loud and boisterous personalities may not seem like good candidates for supportive ministry. In fact, people who are naturally rambunctious and prone to creating scenes can tend to cause staff infections. But that doesn't mean we automatically discard them. Jesus didn't discard James and John because they were the "Sons of Thunder." Instead, He saw their potential and cultivated it—training and correcting them in love.

Yes, James and John would have been a liability if they had not grown and changed. But as long as James and John yielded to the right influence, they were able to channel their powerful personality into a powerful force for God.

James and John: Under the Wrong Influence

In addition to occasionally allowing their personality to get the best of them, James and John also yielded to an ungodly spiritual influence and had to be corrected by Jesus.

James and John were among the disciples whom Jesus sent out to preach the Gospel and heal the sick under the anointing of the Holy Spirit. Along with the others, they experienced spiritual power over demonic forces. However, there was a time when they went out on another type of mission, and, on this occasion, instead of exercising dominion over the devil, they were influenced by the wrong spirit.

LUKE 9:51–56

51 Now it came to pass, when the time had come for Him to be received up, that He steadfastly set His face to go to Jerusalem,

52 and sent messengers before His face. And as they went, they entered a village of the Samaritans, to prepare for Him.

53 But they did not receive Him, because His face was set for the journey to Jerusalem.

54 And when His disciples James and John saw this, they said, "LORD, DO YOU WANT US TO COMMAND FIRE TO COME DOWN FROM HEAVEN AND CONSUME THEM, JUST AS ELIJAH DID?"

55 BUT HE TURNED AND REBUKED THEM, AND SAID, "YOU DO NOT KNOW WHAT MANNER OF SPIRIT YOU ARE OF.

56 For the Son of Man did not come to destroy men's lives but to save them." And they went to another village.

Obviously, Jesus was discerning enough to realize that James' and John's reaction had not been influenced by the Holy Spirit. In correcting them, Jesus directed them to His true purpose and mission. He wasn't going to let them interject a false, corrupt agenda into His ministry. Jesus was determined to keep his staff healthy.

The Right Influence Leads to Health

In James 3:15–18, the other James (the Lord's brother) contrasted two types of influences under which people operate. One of these influences will create a healthy and vibrant staff. The other influence goes hand-in-hand with staff infection.

James accurately described the *cause* of staff infection when he referred to those who are motivated by the *"earthly, sensual, and demonic,"* and James described the *symptoms* of staff infection when he said, *"For where envy and self-seeking exist, confusion and every evil thing are there"* (James 3:15–16). Supportive ministers who are motivated or influenced by earthly, sensual, or demonic desires will cause an outbreak of staff infection, which will result in one or more people exhibiting signs of envy, self-seeking behavior, confusion, and every evil work.

In contrast, the cause of staff *health* is the *"wisdom that is from above"* (James 3:17). This wisdom is *"pure, then peaceable, gentle, willing to yield, full of mercy and good fruits, without partiality and without hypocrisy"*(James 3:17). Supportive ministers who are influenced by godly wisdom will have a strong immunity to staff infection, and these healthy ministers will exhibit signs of purity, peace, gentleness, a willingness to yield, mercy, good fruits, and the ability to minister without hypocrisy.

Doubting Thomas Diagnosed

In addition to dealing with the carnality and the wrong spiritual influences manifested by Peter, James, and John, Jesus was also confronted by Thomas' negativity. When Jesus announced that He was going to go raise Lazarus from the dead, it meant going back to Judea, the place where Jesus had faced bitter opposition (see John 7:1). At Jesus' announcement, Thomas said to the rest of the disciples, "Come along. We might as well die with him" (John 11:16 *Message*). Thomas was not making a statement of consecration and dedication. Thomas was being a wet blanket, soaking the staff with a dose of pessimism.

I personally believe Peter was sincere when he tried to correct Jesus, but he was also sincerely wrong. I'm sure that James and John felt that their anger toward the Samaritans was justified, but Jesus refused to let it become part of His ministry's agenda. Had Thomas been confronted about his pessimism, he may have tried to side-step the issue, claiming that he was simply being realistic. There are times when people who are causing problems actually feel they are doing the right thing, when in fact, their words and actions are causing damage to the Body of Christ.

There is a tendency in human nature to see ourselves, our intentions, and our actions through the filter of self-justification. Proverbs teaches us that *"every way of a man is right in his own eyes..."* (Prov. 21:2), and that *"there is a way that seems right to a man, But its end is the way of death"* (Prov. 16:25). We must always be on guard against deception.

Are You Healed and Whole?

The lesson in all of this is clear. Jesus' own disciples fell prey to staff infection! If Jesus' top staff members could inadvertently yield to and project the wrong spirit, convey the wrong attitude, and attempt to insert a counterfeit agenda into the plan of God, couldn't *we* unknowingly do the same in our various settings today? We, too, need to make sure that we maintain godly motivations—that it is genuinely the Holy Spirit's influence at work in our lives. When we operate under His influence, then we will see *His* fruit—the fruit of the Spirit—abounding in our lives, ministries, and relationships.

The good news about Jesus' disciples is that when they made mistakes, they received correction from Jesus and ultimately moved beyond their mistakes. They learned, they grew, and they matured—*and* they got healed of staff infection! We must endeavor to do the same.

There are different influences vying for control in our life. We can choose to yield to wrong influences—to the devil or to the carnal nature. Or we can choose to yield to the Holy Spirit and to allow His influence to mold and shape our life.

One of the most important things we can ever do is to really embrace what it means to "follow Jesus." If we are going to fulfill God's plan for our life and become the supportive ministers God wants us to be, we must focus entirely on Jesus and make Him our foundation for every value, belief, thought, and action.

QUESTIONS FOR REFLECTION AND DISCUSSION

1. Jesus' disciples were often competitive instead of cooperative. Instead of seeking to serve, they sought to be exalted. Would other people consider you competitive or cooperative?
2. In what ways are you seeking to serve? In what ways might you be seeking to exalt yourself?
3. Does it bother you when other people get recognized or rewarded?
4. Do you have a tendency to focus on other people instead of on fulfilling your own calling?
5. Does your personality tend to get you into trouble?
6. What parts of your personality do you need to yield to the Holy Spirit and allow Him to soften or reshape?
7. In what ways can you relate to the mistakes of Peter, James, John, and Thomas?
8. Do you believe that you consistently yield to the influence of the Holy Spirit and project His influence toward others?
9. Under which of the two influences described in James 3:15–18 do you more consistently function? Has there ever been a time when you operated under the wrong influence described in this passage of scripture.
10. Looking back, have you ever had a wrong attitude or ever acted wrongly, but thought at the time that what you were doing was right?
11. Looking at yourself today, is it possible that your current attitudes or actions may need adjusting, especially if you took away the filter of self-justification? If so, how can you recover yourself and get back on the right track?
12. What did you learn from this chapter and how can you apply it?
13. What areas do you need to pray about or improve in?

Know Who
You Work For

When God spoke to Moses out of the burning bush, calling him to deliver the children of Israel from Egypt, Moses expressed to God a number of concerns and insecurities. One of Moses' concerns had to do with his perceived lack of speaking ability. God responded to Moses' concern in Exodus 4:14–16.

EXODUS 4:14–16

14 So the anger of the Lord was kindled against Moses, and He said: "Is not Aaron the Levite your brother? I know that he can speak well. And look, he is also coming out to meet you. When he sees you, he will be glad in his heart.

15 Now you shall speak to him and put the words in his mouth. And I will be with your mouth and with his mouth, and I will teach you what you shall do.

16 So he shall be your spokesman to the people. And he himself shall be as a mouth for you, and you shall be to him as God."

In this passage, God explains the plan He has designed for Moses' brother Aaron. Aaron's role couldn't have been clearer. He was to be an extension of Moses—a representative. Aaron wasn't assigned to work *for the people*; he was supposed to work *for Moses.*

But what happened when the pressure came? Did Aaron faithfully represent Moses and act on his behalf? Was Aaron a healthy part of Moses' staff, or did he come down with a bad case of staff infection? Let's study what the Bible has to say about Aaron's working relationship with Moses.

Representing the People
Instead of the Leader

First, let's see what happened when the people asked Aaron to make them an idol. At the time, Moses was up on the mountain, receiving the Ten Commandments from the Lord. In his absence, the children of Israel began to grow restless and to bombard Aaron with complaints about Moses and with requests for Aaron to take action.

Exodus 32:1 says, *"Now when the people saw that Moses delayed coming down from the mountain, the people gathered together to Aaron, and said to him, 'Come, make us gods that shall go before us; for as for this Moses, the man who brought us up out of the land of Egypt, we do not know what has become of him.'"* This would have been a great opportunity for Aaron to be Moses' representative spokesman. It was his chance to do the job he'd been assigned—to support Moses and to speak on Moses' behalf in accordance with *Moses'* vision and assignment from God.

Aaron chose to go his own way and do his own thing. Instead of defending and representing Moses to the people, Aaron did something totally opposite.

EXODUS 32:2–6

2 **And Aaron said to them, "Break off the golden earrings which are in the ears of your wives, your sons, and your daughters, and bring them to me."**

3 **So all the people broke off the golden earrings which were in their ears, and brought them to Aaron.**

4   And he received the gold from their hand, and he
     fashioned it with an engraving tool, and made a mold-
     ed calf. Then they said, "This is your god, O Israel,
     that brought you out of the land of Egypt!"
5   So when Aaron saw it, he built an altar before it. And
     Aaron made a proclamation and said, "Tomorrow is a
     feast to the Lord."
6   Then they rose early on the next day, offered burnt
     offerings, and brought peace offerings; and the people
     sat down to eat and drink, and rose up to play.

Instead of being a positive influence *upon* the people (by
representing and reflecting Moses), Aaron yielded to the negative influence *of* the people. In other words, Aaron carried out
the people's vision instead of carrying out the vision God had
given Moses.

Aaron should have functioned as Moses' representative
and exerted influence toward the people on Moses' behalf.
Aaron could have at least tried to keep them on track as they
waited for Moses' return, but he didn't. What went wrong?
Where did Aaron's spiritual immune system break down?
Had he lost confidence in Moses' leadership? Could he only
function well when Moses was right there beside him? Did
Aaron value favor with the people above his assignment? Was
popularity more important to him than principle? Why did
Aaron fail to lead? What caused him to yield to popular
opinion?

Aaron's Primary Mistake

I don't think making the golden calf under the influence
of the people was Aaron's first mistake. I believe Aaron had
already missed it—when he failed to proactively and regularly
articulate Moses' vision to the people. This primary mistake
(failing to proactively and regularly articulate Moses' vision)
led to the people's eventual demand for an idol, and it was

this primary mistake that led to Aaron's mistaken surrender to the people's demands.

> IF AARON HAD BEEN ACTIVELY PURSUING THE PLAN OF GOD AS GIVEN TO MOSES, HE WOULD HAVE NEVER ALLOWED THE PEOPLE TO PURSUE THEIR UNGODLY PLAN.

Let me explain what I mean. What was Aaron doing the entire time Moses was up on the mountain with God? Was he actively reinforcing Moses' vision, reminding the people of their destiny and their divine calling? I don't think he was. Had this divine plan been firmly rooted in the forefront of the people's thinking, I doubt they would have been clamoring for a golden calf. *And*, had God's plan been on the forefront of *Aaron's* thinking, I don't think he would have so readily yielded to such an ungodly demand.

I believe Aaron had shifted into a passive style of leadership (which is not really "leadership" at all) long before the incident with the golden calf. If Aaron had been actively pursuing the plan of God as given to Moses, he would have never allowed the people to pursue their ungodly plan.

Don't allow people and their opposing agendas get you offtrack. If you are a church leader, your job is to represent the pastor and to carry out your assignment in conjunction with his overall vision. If you lose sight of that vision, you will more susceptible to embracing and promoting other visions as they come along.

Excuses, Excuses!

We get more insight into Aaron's mistakes and problems by studying the conversation he had with Moses when Moses confronted him about the calf. As you read the following account of the confrontation, keep in mind that the Bible explicitly says Aaron *"received the gold from their hand, and he fashioned it with an engraving tool, and made a molded calf"* (Exod. 32:4). In other words, Aaron used an engraving tool to form and fashion (or sculpt) a calf out of the melted gold, which he himself had melted down.

EXODUS 32:22–24

22 So Aaron said, "Do not let the anger of my lord become hot. You know the people, that they are set on evil.

23 "For they said to me, 'Make us gods that shall go before us; as for this Moses, the man who brought us out of the land of Egypt, we do not know what has become of him.'

24 "AND I SAID TO THEM, 'WHOEVER HAS ANY GOLD, LET THEM BREAK IT OFF.' SO THEY GAVE IT TO ME, AND I CAST IT INTO THE FIRE, AND THIS CALF CAME OUT."

In verse 24, Aaron tries to convince Moses that the calf made itself! That Aaron just collected the gold and threw it into the fire–and *poof!* out came this calf! Aaron never took responsibility for his actions. In this situation, Aaron forfeited his role as a leader and became a blame-shifter. He blamed the people for their behavior when, in fact, *he* was to blame for not having done his job. The very next verse says that, "Moses saw that the people were running wild and that Aaron had let them get out of control and so become a laughing-stock to their enemies" (Exod. 32:25 *NIV*).

It's unfortunate that the vision God gave Moses had not taken root in the people or in Aaron–the one chosen to represent Moses. How could Aaron accurately represent Moses, if Aaron did not firmly grasp the vision he was supposed to be representing? A successful supportive minister *must* know and embrace the leader's vision in order to accurately present that vision and keep it before the people.

If you are a supportive minister, it's important that you carry within your heart the vision of the church. The vision includes the values, priorities, and goals which the pastor has presented for the congregation. Help your pastor to carry out the vision and to communicate it to others so they in turn can have a part in carrying it out.

QUESTIONS FOR REFLECTION AND DISCUSSION

1. Do you see yourself as working for the pastor or working for the people?
2. Have you ever felt pressure to step away from the vision of the church in order to be popular with people?
3. In what ways do you proactively live out and communicate the vision of the church? How do you keep the vision in the forefront of your mind and in the mind of people?
4. Instead of addressing or correcting an issue that could be nipped in the bud, so to speak, have you ever waited until it became a full-blown problem before you did anything? What would have been a better way to handle that situation?
5. Describe a situation where you took responsibility for a mistake instead of shifting blame.
6. Can you think of a situation where you shifted blame for a mistake instead of taking responsibility?
7. What did you learn from this chapter and how can you apply it?
8. What areas do you need to pray about or improve in?

Offense Can Kill You

O ne of the most intriguing stories in the Bible—although it is rarely addressed—is that of Ahithophel in the Old Testament. In this chapter, we'll only study a few aspects of the story, but I encourage you to read it in its entirety. (See 2 Samuel 15:12–17:23.)

Ahithophel was an advisor to David and later to David's son Absalom. Second Samuel 16:23 says, *"Now the advice of Ahithophel, which he gave in those days, was as if one had inquired at the oracle of God. So was all the advice of Ahithophel both with David and with Absalom."* Ahithophel was highly regarded for his wisdom and insight, but he lacked loyalty in a most glaring way. When Absalom led his infamous rebellion against his father the king, Ahithophel quickly abandoned David and joined Absalom's insurrection.

As David was fleeing the uprising, he realized that the greatest danger he faced was the strength Absalom would gain from receiving Ahithophel's wise counsel. To counter the wisdom of his former advisor, David sent his loyal friend Hushai into the court of Absalom to feign loyalty to Absalom and to contradict whatever counsel Ahithophel might offer.

When Ahithophel advised Absalom to pursue and kill David without delay, Hushai gave the opposite advice: "Wait until you get the country fully behind you, then pursue David" (2 Sam. 17:7–11). Much to Ahithophel's dismay, his counsel was rejected in favor of Hushai's advice.

Ahithophel's reaction to this rejection was extreme.

2 SAMUEL 17:23

23 Now when Ahithophel saw that his advice was not followed, he saddled a donkey, and arose and went home to his house, to his city. Then he put his household in order, and HANGED HIMSELF, AND DIED; and he was buried in his father's tomb.

We've only scratched the surface of this story, but it's still astonishing how volatile Ahithophel became when his advice was not followed. He was devastated by the rejection to the point of taking his own life. However, there's more to this story than Ahithophel's feelings being hurt over this isolated incident of advice not taken.

Perhaps Ahithophel knew that by ignoring this initial advice, Absalom was starting down the wrong course. Perhaps Ahithophel could foresee that this wrong course would eventually cause the insurrection to fail, leaving Ahithophel to face the shame and disgrace of being on the wrong side of the rebellion. But I believe there's even more to this story.

The Root of Offense

Ahithophel most likely lost his sense of objectivity in this entire matter due to an offense he had been carrying for years. The Bible tells us that King David committed adultery with Bathsheba, got her pregnant, and then had her husband Uriah killed. It appears from Scripture that Ahithophel was the grandfather of Bathsheba (2 Sam. 11:3; 23:34). David corrupted Ahithophel's granddaughter and murdered Ahithophel's grandson-in-law, then Ahithophel's great-grandson died as a consequence of David's actions.

It seems that Ahithophel was never able to get over the offense David caused by his flagrant sins. The depth of Ahithophel's offense toward David is evi-

> AHITHOPHEL ALLOWED THE WORST IN DAVID TO BRING OUT THE WORST IN HIM.

denced by the fact that he volunteered to personally lead twelve thousand soldiers to hunt and kill David without delay.

Ahithophel had served David for years and had given him counsel that was "...as wise as though it had come directly from the mouth of God" (2 Sam. 16:23 *NLT*). And yet, in spite of Ahithophel's wisdom that helped David, offense was lurking beneath the surface—festering with the worst kind of infection imaginable. It was an infection that nearly killed David and ended up destroying Ahithophel.

Ironically, in the Hebrew language the name "Ahithophel" means *brother of folly*.[1] Ahithophel offered great wisdom in his counsel, but he was unable to live out that wisdom in his own life. David was wrong in what he did concerning Bathsheba and Uriah; there is no justifying or sugar-coating his actions. But Ahithophel allowed the worst in David to bring out the worst in him. He allowed sin in David to bring out sin in his own life, and he allowed David's carnality to bring out his own carnality.

Guard Against Offense

We can learn many valuable lessons from Ahithophel that will help us in our personal life and in ministry.

First, *we must guard ourselves against offense*. It is a dangerous infection that can contaminate us and spread to others. The background issues in Ahithophel's story are extreme, and, from a human standpoint, the offense is understandable. David sinned greatly, and the effects of his sin greatly impacted

Ahithophel's life and family. However, as justified as his offense might seem, Ahithophel suffered—and ultimately died—because he would not let it go.

However, as justified as his offense might seem, Ahithophel suffered—and ultimately died—because he would not let it go.

While Ahithophel's offense seemed justified, many people in churches today allow offense to take root over trivial matters. Attitudes get totally out of line over small, petty issues that are insignificant compared to God's overall purpose. Offense produces ugly results whether the occasion for the offense was large or small. Offense of any kind, "justifiable" or not, will eventually hurt you and the people around you.

Not everyone who becomes offended is going to take part in an outright rebellion the way Ahithophel did, but symptoms of staff infection can manifest in other ways. Some people become passive aggressive in that they *say* everything is fine, but in their heart, attitude, and actions they've put on the brakes. They may still serve and "keep up appearances," but they no longer serve wholeheartedly. Other passive aggressive people may begin to sulk, pout, and withdraw. Whether offense plays out with aggression or with passive aggression, it's still offense and still rebellion and still harmful.

Your Advice Won't Always Be Taken

We've learned from Ahithophel's mistakes that we must guard against offense. Second, we need to learn that *our advice won't always be accepted*. Not everything in life will be done the way we think it should be done. And that's okay!

Remember, if there are 250 people in a church, there are probably 250 opinions (or more)! If you give input and it is not accepted, how will you respond? Don't take it personally if your opinion or ideas are not embraced. If you are going to be part of a healthy team, it's important to maintain respect and cooperativeness even when you disagree with a decision. You must be willing to give 100 percent effort even when you don't agree 100 percent.

Offense is a dangerous tool of the enemy—dangerous because of the damage it causes and more dangerous because it's often subtle and hard to detect. If you have held onto offense (deemed justifiable or not), let it go before it harms you or spreads staff infection to others. Furthermore, make it your aim and goal to never be the cause of offense in another person's life. Offense can kill people, churches, and ministries in no time at all.

QUESTIONS FOR REFLECTION AND DISCUSSION

1. Have you ever felt "justified" in being offended. What did you do to uproot the offense?
2. Have you ever been the occasion of someone else being offended? What did you do to restore the relationship?
3. Have you ever allowed the worst in someone else to bring out the worst in you? Have you ever allowed the sin of another to get you into sin? Have you ever allowed the carnality of someone else to bring out the carnality in you? What did you do to get back on the right track?
4. When you offer input or advice and it is not accepted, how do you respond?
5. What did you learn from this chapter and how can you apply it?
6. What areas do you need to pray about or improve in?

---

[1] James Strong, "Hebrew and Chaldee Dictionary," *The New Strong's Exhaustive Concordance of the Bible* (Nashville: Thomas Nelson, 1984), 10.

Absalom: The Ultimate Staff Infection

A final example of staff infection, and perhaps the worst kind of all, involves David's son Absalom. Some of the other types of infection we've studied might be considered less sinister because of the *motivation* behind them. For example, Peter's trying to counsel Jesus in Matthew chapter 16 or Aaron's yielding to the influence of the people in Exodus chapter 32 could be described as somewhat inadvertent. Peter was doing what seemed right to him, and Aaron simply yielded to pressure from others. However, what Absalom did was calculated, deliberate, and premeditated.

If the infection that contaminated Ahithophel was his offense over something David *had done* (adultery and murder), then Absalom's infection was rooted in the offense he took concerning something David *had neglected to do* (not taking action over the rape of Tamar).

Second Samuel chapter 13 tells the story of Absalom's beautiful sister Tamar. We read that Tamar was raped by her half-brother Amnon and that King David (their father) was angry about it (v. 21). However, there is no indication that David ever took any action against Amnon. Two years after the incident, Absalom took matters into his own hands and avenged the rape of Tamar by having Amnon killed.

Following an extended time in exile, Absalom eventually went back to Jerusalem, but his relationship with David remained strained. Though there appeared to be a reconciliation in Second Samuel 14:33, Absalom's eventual rebellion makes it clear that the offense was never really resolved.

Second Samuel chapter 15 describes how Absalom's rebellion started. Absalom slowly began to pull the hearts of the people away from King David by promising them the justice they sought.

2 SAMUEL 15:1–6

1   After this it happened that Absalom provided himself with chariots and horses, and fifty men to run before him.

2   Now Absalom would rise early and stand beside the way to the gate. So it was, whenever anyone who had a lawsuit came to the king for a decision, that Absalom would call to him and say, "What city are you from?" And he would say, "Your servant is from such and such a tribe of Israel."

3   Then Absalom would say to him, "Look, your case is good and right; but there is no deputy of the king to hear you."

4   Moreover Absalom would say, "Oh, that I were made judge in the land, and everyone who has any suit or cause would come to me; then I would give him justice."

5   And so it was, whenever anyone came near to bow down to him, that he would put out his hand and take him and kiss him.

6   In this manner Absalom acted toward all Israel who came to the king for judgment. So Absalom stole the hearts of the men of Israel.

Verse 6 says that Absalom "stole the hearts of the men of Israel." It's interesting that the Bible uses the word "stole," which implies that Absalom gained their allegiance by dishonest means. What Absalom promised the people may have sounded noble and just, but there was nothing noble or just about the way Absalom went about subverting David's authority.

> WHAT ABSALOM PROMISED THE PEOPLE MAY HAVE SOUNDED NOBLE AND JUST, BUT THERE WAS NOTHING NOBLE OR JUST ABOUT THE WAY ABSALOM WENT ABOUT SUBVERTING DAVID'S AUTHORITY.

We can detect several of Absalom's character traits in this passage in Second Samuel chapter 15:

- Absalom harbored offense because of David's lack of action against Amnon.
- Absalom was a proud and vain man.
- Absalom was a flatterer.
- Absalom was an opportunist.
- Absalom undermined David's authority while simultaneously building his own following.

Let's briefly examine each of these traits and see how they operated in Absalom's life and affected the people around him.

Harbored Offense Toward David

Absalom harbored offense because of David's lack of action against Amnon. This early offense laid the groundwork for Absalom's later complaint, *"Oh, that I were made judge in the land, and everyone who has any suit or cause would come to me; then I would give him justice"* (2 Sam. 15:4). In effect, Absalom was saying, "The leader isn't doing things right, but I would if I were in charge." While Absalom's initial anger over David's inaction concerning the rape of Tamar may have been justified, we still come back to the basic principle that two wrongs don't make a right. David was wrong, but so was Absalom because he a) harbored offense in his heart and b) eventually acted upon it.

Proud and Vain

Absalom was also a proud and vain man. He loved drawing attention to himself. Second Samuel 15:1 says, *"Absalom provided himself with chariots and horses, and fifty men to run before him."* Can you imagine the scene? Riding through the city with chariots and horses and *fifty* men running ahead to signal your arrival?

Absalom's vanity is also seen in Second Samuel 14:25–26.

2 SAMUEL 14:25–26

25 Now in all Israel there was no one who was praised as much as Absalom for his good looks. From the sole of his foot to the crown of his head there was no blemish in him.

26 And when he cut the hair of his head—at the end of every year he cut it because it was heavy on him—when he cut it, he weighed the hair of his head....

Do you know anyone who *weighs* their hair after they cut it? Yes, it would be difficult to stay humble if you were the most praised person in the entire nation, but this seems like an unusual amount of self-interest. Absalom tried to justify his actions in Second Samuel 15:1–6 by claiming to be a proponent for justice, but I'm sure ego was a central part of his behavior.

A Flatterer

Absalom was a flatterer. Second Samuel 15:3 says, *"Then Absalom would say to him, 'Look, your case is good and right.'"* Absalom flattered people to win their favor and pull them over to his side. The Bible does not speak highly of flatterers. Psalm 12:2 refers unfavorably to those who speak with *"flattering lips and a double heart."* And Jude 16 harshly describes those who *"...flatter others to get favors in return"* (*NLT*).

Have you ever heard it said, "Flattery will get you nowhere"? It's usually said by someone who's just been flattered, and he is letting the flatterer know that sweet talk won't accomplish anything. However, this statement is not completely true; in this world, flattery *will* get you somewhere. But the place it takes you (as the flatterer or as those who let flattery puff them up) is not the place God wants you to go.

An Opportunist

Absalom was an opportunist who appealed to the disgruntled. He exploited imperfections (real or imagined) within David's kingdom to accentuate and further cultivate discontent among the people.

Are you an opportunist? Are you appealing to the disgruntled members of your church or organization? A good way to tell is by noticing the effect your words and actions are having on the people around you. Are the people being pushed toward supporting the pastor or leader? Or are they being pulled away from the pastor in support of you?

Undermined Authority

Absalom undermined David's authority in order to carry out his own agenda. Absalom tore down the image of the king and simultaneously worked to build a following around himself. Paul's warning to the Ephesian elders was reminiscent of Absalom's conduct: *"For I know this, that after my departure savage wolves will come in among you, not sparing the flock. Also from among yourselves men will rise up, speaking perverse things, to draw away the disciples after themselves"* (Acts 20:29–30).

Speaking of Absalom's behavior, one author wrote:

> In the spiritual realm, a man who will lead a rebellion has already proven, no matter how grandiose his words or angelic his ways, that he has a critical nature, an unprincipled character, and hidden motives in his heart. Frankly, he is a thief. He creates dissatisfaction and tension within the realm, and then either seizes power or siphons off followers. The followers he gets, he uses to found his own dominion. Such a sorry beginning, built on the foundation of insurrection... No, God never honors division in His realm. I find it

curious that men who feel qualified to split God's kingdom do not feel capable of going somewhere else, to another land, to raise up a completely new kingdom. No, they must steal from another leader. I have never seen the exception. They seem always to need at least a few pre-packaged followers.[1]

Absalom surely was a thief, in that he "stole the hearts of the people" away from David. Are you doing or saying anything that would steal people's allegiance away from your pastor?

Don't Sow Discord

Throughout *In Search of Timothy*, we have been studying various supportive ministers in order to learn from them—some teach us what *to do* and some teach us what *not to do*. In studying Second Samuel 15:1–6 and in analyzing several of Absalom's *negative* character traits, we are definitely creating a list for ourselves of *what not to do*.

Many churches have experienced harmful and unnecessary splits because a person or a group began focusing on some type of imperfection or deficiency in the church or in the pastor. It's important to realize that as long as there are human beings in the Church, there will always be faults, flaws, and imperfections. The ability to find a flaw is no great virtue or talent. There were problems before you arrived at the church; there will be problems while you are there; and there will be problems after you're gone. We are all imperfect and in the process of improving.

I believe that the number-one weapon Satan uses against supportive ministers is to get them into criticism and fault-finding. We must realize that God has called us to be part of the *answer*, not the *problem*. We will never solve anything by stirring up division and strife; in fact, we will only cause more problems.

In Proverbs 6:16–19, God lists seven things that He hates—things that are an abomination to Him. The last of these is *"one who sows discord among brethren"* (v. 19). Other words for "discord" are dissension, conflict, and friction. When people are offended, they often want to share that offense with others. They want people to sympathize with them, feel sorry for them, and take sides with them against the pastor (or whoever offended them). Instead of dealing with the issue in a constructive manner, these people choose to *sow discord among the brethren.* An isolated infection is never good, but one that spreads to other parts of the body is even worse.

I believe that a noble and virtuous supportive minister is one who will give his very best in spite of imperfections. He will be mindful of the fact that not only is the pastor (or church) imperfect, but so is he. We must have our minds made-up that we are not going to allow the enemy to use us to create strife and division in the church. We're going to be part of the solution instead of the problem. We will be counted among the peacemakers whom Jesus said are blessed (Matt. 5:9).

Measure yourself against the list of Absalom's character traits, as described in this chapter. Are any of these traits present in your own character? If so, then dig a little deeper, allowing the light of God's Word and Spirit to illuminate the root cause of these destructive traits. Should you find a seed of offense hiding anywhere in your heart, weed it out before it grows into an infection that spreads throughout the Body.

QUESTIONS FOR REFLECTION AND DISCUSSION

1. When you notice deficiencies or imperfections in the church or in people, what do you do to keep criticism from taking root in you?
2. What do you do to ensure that you will take things in stride and keep your heart and attitude right?

3. When you encounter critical and disgruntled people, how do you encourage them to be positive and productive?
4. Are you confident that your efforts are building the Kingdom and not building a personal following?
5. Are you confident that you are a peacemaker and not one who sows discord among the people ?
6. What did you learn from this chapter and how can you apply it?
7. What areas do you need to pray about or improve in?

---

[1] Gene Edwards, *A Tale of Three Kings* (Augusta, ME: Christian Books, 1980), 67–68. Used by permission of the publisher.

PART V

Where to Find Timothy

Throughout this book, we have studied various biblical principles and examples of supportive ministry, the traits great supportive ministers possess, and exactly what supportive ministers ought *not* to do and be. Now that we know that "Timothy" is the kind of supportive minister every pastor wants to find and the kind we should all want to be, where do we search for him?

In this final section of *In Search of Timothy*, I want to speak directly to two groups of people: the pastors or leaders who are searching to *employ* this Timothy and the people who are searching to *become* this Timothy. I trust these final words of encouragement and instruction will help you in find and cultivate the minister you are looking for.

The Man in the Mirror

This chapter is written to pastors and leaders (even department heads and supervisors)—the ones who are searching for Timothy because they want him to join their staff. Before pastors or leaders start searching high and low for Timothy, they first need to look in the mirror to make sure they embody these "Timothy" attributes themselves. Leaders will attract more of who they are. If *they* don't exemplify any of Timothy's traits, why would their staff or church members?

Although *In Search of Timothy* is primarily geared toward supportive ministers, its principles still apply to pastors. Every pastor and leader has or should have a pastor or leader of their own that they are submitted to or mentored by. The principles in this book can help you become a better Timothy to that person or organization.

As I said in the preface, the content I have presented are *ideals* for which we should strive. However, we are all at different levels of growth, maturity, and development. This book is not meant to be a tool for leaders to rigidly measure their staff against. Rather, it is a call for *everyone* to look within himself and grow in godly character and ministerial effectiveness.

Pastors, be patient with your staff and church members. Treat them with kindness. Remember how Rehoboam's influence was drastically diminished because he lacked diplomacy in dealing with people. Second Chronicles 10:7 says, "If you will be a servant to this people, be considerate of their needs and respond with compassion, work things out with them, they'll end up doing anything for you" (*Message*).

Do you want supportive ministers who will "do anything for you"? Then be considerate of their needs and respond to them with compassion. Encourage every sign of growth and be long-suffering toward them. Barnabas didn't give up on Mark; he cultivated the potential within him. Jesus didn't give up on Peter, James, and John when they made mistakes, and Paul didn't give up on Timothy when he had shortcomings. These leaders continued to lead their supportive ministers by example and to instruct them, pray for them, encourage them, and love them.

Paul's Pattern of Leadership

If leaders want their supportive ministers to be like Timothy, it's a good idea for leaders to be like Paul. Therefore, let's briefly study Paul's pattern of leadership:

1. *Lead by Example.* Paul modeled the kind of ministry he wanted to see in others.
2. *Establish a Partnership.* Paul worked with his supportive ministers, looked out for their best interests, and gave them instructions and guidelines.
3. *Remain Connected.* Paul still gave guidelines and feedback to his protégés even when they ministered in a location without him. He continued to minister to them even when they were apart.

As we look more in-depth at each of these principles, we can see how they ought to play out in our relationship with supportive ministers.

Number One:
Lead by Example

Good leaders lead by example. I feel sure the Apostle Paul embodied (or was at least growing) in the traits that he instructed Timothy to possess. I also believe that Paul was the leader he was training Timothy to be. It is important for leaders to model the kind of ministry they want to see in their supportive ministers. Of all people, preachers should practice what they preach and not be caught living by the motto, "Do as I say, not as I do."

Paul understood the power of example, and he purposely presented himself as a model to be emulated.

1 CORINTHIANS 4:16
16 Therefore I urge you, imitate me.

1 CORINTHIANS 11:1
1   Imitate me, just as I also imitate Christ.

PHILIPPIANS 3:17
17 Brethren, join in following my example, and note those who so walk, as you have us for a pattern.

PHILIPPIANS 4:9
9   The things which you learned and received and heard and saw in me, these do, and the God of peace will be with you.

2 TIMOTHY 3:10,14
10 But you have carefully followed my doctrine, manner of life, purpose, faith, longsuffering, love, perseverance....
14 But you must continue in the things which you have learned and been assured of, knowing from whom you have learned them.

Even though he admonished believers to imitate his example, Paul realized he wasn't perfect, and he recognized that he always had room to grow. He knew that he himself was a work in progress. He said, *"Not that I have already attained, or am already perfected; but I press on, that I may lay hold of that for which Christ Jesus has also laid hold*

> PAUL WAS MINDFUL OF THE GRACE AND MERCY OF GOD THAT HAD BEEN EXTENDED TOWARD HIM, AND HE, IN TURN, EXTENDED THE SAME TO TIMOTHY.

of me. Brethren, I do not count myself to have apprehended; but one thing I do, forgetting those things which are behind and reaching forward to those things which are ahead, I press toward the goal for the prize of the upward call of God in Christ Jesus" (Phil. 3:12–14).

Paul was mindful of the grace and mercy of God that had been extended toward him, and he, in turn, extended the same to Timothy. As we read his letters to Timothy, we don't see Paul demanding instant and absolute perfection from Timothy, but we see him encouraging, guiding, nurturing, and cultivating the gifts within Timothy. We see Paul admonishing Timothy and instructing him toward maturity and effectiveness, even in spite of Timothy's weaknesses and the areas where he struggled.

Number Two:
Establish a Partnership

It's been said, "You can employ men and hire hands to work *for* you, but you must win their hearts to have them work *with* you." [1] You win people's hearts by loving them, which means you pray for them, you listen to them, and you build them up. The bottom line is–*you care about your people.*

Pastors: supportive ministers need to know that you have their best interests at heart and that you aren't just using them to get a job done. Follow Paul's example in establishing a partnership with your supportive ministers and in looking out for their best interests. As you read of Paul's leadership toward his sons in the faith, you can't help but notice a great depth of love and affection that he had for them. He didn't see Timothy,

Titus, and others in a merely utilitarian way. They weren't just objects to be used for his own gain or for the fulfillment of his ministry. Rather, they were truly beloved sons, and he cared about their well-being.

Paul went so far as to write ahead to churches to instruct them on how to properly receive and treat Timothy, making sure Timothy was well-protected and cared for. Although it is accurate to say that Timothy was Paul's apprentice or protégé, Timothy also became Paul's partner in ministry, working with Paul for the same cause and with the same heart.

Another way Paul looked out for Timothy and cared for him was by giving him clear and thorough instructions (which is what the pastoral epistles are all about). Paul did not assume that Timothy would intuitively have all the ministerial knowledge he needed to be effective. Paul believed it was necessary to give Timothy ample instructions and guidelines. The instructions Paul gave were an investment in Timothy's development.

Number Three:
Remain Connected

Have you ever felt like you and your staff were on two opposing teams instead of on the same team? Leaders and their staff members sometimes become disconnected and even adversarial. When this happens, they may begin to point fingers instead of viewing their relationship as a connected partnership. Hall of Fame coach Bear Bryant presented the solution to this problem when he said, "If anything goes bad, *I* did it. If anything goes semi-good, then *we* did it. If anything goes real good, then *you* did it. That's all it takes to get people to win football games for you."[2]

Leaders must consistently encourage their team. Praise what's right and correct what's wrong, but don't create an atmosphere where people are afraid to fail. Let them know you are not just their coach—you are their biggest fan. And you are all on the same team!

Paul remained connected with his supportive ministers throughout his life. He recognized that training supportive ministers is an ongoing cultivation that does not end. Paul was patient with Timothy throughout this entire learning process and provided Timothy with inspiration and information on an ongoing basis. Even when Paul was nearing his death, he continued to pour into Timothy's life and supply him with vital instruction on how he could fulfill his ministry.

Minister Motivated by Love

Paul selflessly ministered to Timothy and to everyone else. He gave to them from the love of God within him. He did *not* give because he wanted them to reciprocate his kindness (which they often did not do). Paul told the Corinthians: *"I will not be burdensome to you; for I do not seek yours, but you. For the children ought not to lay up for the parents, but the parents for the children. And I will very gladly spend and be spent for your souls; though the more abundantly I love you, the less I am loved"* (2 Cor. 12:14–15).

Paul operated under the assumption that he would give more to the Corinthians than he would necessarily receive from them. He was able to do this because he sought the good of the people to whom he ministered instead of seeking to receive good from them. Motivated by love, Paul tirelessly trained and ministered to others.

Paul grew beyond expecting equal reciprocation for his giving. He didn't become bitter or disillusioned by the inequality of the matter. He had the attitude that he must do the right thing whether anyone else responded appropriately or not.

This principle of doing right regardless of what other people do was poignantly illustrated in this sign hanging on the wall of the children's home run by Mother Teresa in Calcutta:

People are often unreasonable, illogical, and self-centered; Forgive them anyway.

If you are kind, people may accuse you of selfish, ulterior motives; Be kind anyway.

If you are successful, you will win some false friends and some true enemies; Succeed anyway.

If you are honest and frank, people may cheat you; Be honest and frank anyway.

What you spend years building, someone could destroy overnight; Build anyway.

If you find serenity and happiness, they may be jealous; Be happy anyway.

The good you do today, people will often forget tomorrow; Do good anyway.

Give the world the best you have, and it may never be enough; Give the world the best that you've got anyway.

You see, in the final analysis, it is between you and God; It was never between you and them anyway.[3]

It's a natural part of life that some of the ministers you train are going to leave and go to work somewhere else. *Train them anyway.*

Keep On Investing

Both Jesus and Paul invested in supportive ministers and in some cases never received the desired return on their investment. Judas never achieved his potential, and Demas left Paul to return to his regular life. But those results didn't cause Jesus or Paul to become jaded or bitter. They continued to sow into people's lives based on the love of God within them.

At some point in their ministry, most leaders will invest in a supportive minister and not receive the benefit from that investment. But even when we don't receive an immediate return on our investment, we must remember that we don't invest in people merely for our own benefit anyway. We invest in people for *their* benefit—so they can grow spiritually and become all that God has called them to be—and for the benefit of the Kingdom of God.

There may be times when the people we train will take that training elsewhere and benefit another church or ministry. Think of those people as seed sown into the Kingdom of God. Even though your church or ministry may not receive the full and immediate benefit, the Kingdom of God overall will receive benefit, and for that, you should be grateful and thankful.

If the supportive ministers you train leave to go work elsewhere, don't become bitter or disillusioned over it. Certainly don't let it stop you from investing in other men and women in your church. As Zig Ziglar once said, "Much worse than training people and losing them is *not* training them and *keeping* them." [4] When you sow workers into the Kingdom (intentionally or not), stay in faith and expect to reap other laborers to take the place of the supportive ministers who have left your church.

Search the Pews

We've seen throughout this book that great leadership is only fully successful when it is accompanied by great followership. However, keep in mind that "following is an act of trust, faith in the course of the leader, and that faith can be generated only if leaders act with integrity." [5] Remember, Paul was a great leader in part because he practiced what he preached and lived by the principles he used to train Timothy. Therefore, the traits of great supportive ministers are also the traits of great leaders. When you embody those traits of honesty, integrity, faithfulness, and so forth, your supportive ministers will be able to trust you and place their faith in the course you set for them to follow.

Perhaps you feel certain that you closely embody the traits of Timothy and you know for a fact that are you treating people well and investing heavily in them. Perhaps you are also following the leadership patterns of Paul, and yet you *still* say, "I need far more help than what I'm getting. I've searched and searched, and I'm still looking for Timothy!"

Be encouraged...and be patient. You don't have to search the world over to find Timothy. You don't necessarily have to attend the graduation ceremonies of various seminaries and Bible schools in the hope of spotting Timothy as he receives his diploma. You may find some great people that way, but perhaps Timothy is sitting in one of your church pews. He may be the one who comes every Sunday and sits quietly with his wife and children. She may be the one who volunteers once a month in the bookstore. They may be the ones who are newly born again but who want to get involved in the church doing anything they can. You may not have to go very far to find Timothy—just look in your own church. You may need to train them, teach them, love them, and lead them, but that's okay. Timothys are made, not born.

QUESTIONS FOR REFLECTION AND DISCUSSION

1. Taking a good look into the figurative mirror, how closely do you resemble the Timothy we've described throughout this book?
2. Have you been expecting your supportive ministers to be something you're not?
3. In what ways do you lead by example?
4. In what ways have you established a partnership with those working under your leadership?
5. In what ways do you remain connected with those you've trained?
6. Have you ever trained people, only to have them leave your church? Were you tempted to feel your time was a wasted investment?
7. List five people in your church who you believe have the potential to become a "Timothy." What can you do to begin cultivating that potential?
8. What did you learn from this chapter and how can you apply it?
9. What areas do you need to pray about or improve in?

[1] Tiorio, as quoted in Ted Goodman, ed., *The Forbes Book of Business Quotations* (New York: Black Dog & Leventhal Publishers, 1997), 242.

[2] As quoted in "Sermon Illustrations, Topic: Credit," Bible.org: Trustworthy Bible Study Resources, http://www.bible.org/illus.asp?topic_id=342.

[3] "Do It Anyway," http://catholicgirl.faithweb.com/mother_teresa.htm.

[4] Duncan Maxwell Anderson, "Creating Loyalty; Zig Ziglar: Discipline Inspires Devotion," *Success Magazine*, November 1994, http://www.mlmhelp.com/library/articles/loyalty.asp.

[5] Lawrence M. Miller, as quoted in "Article Number 172: Ethics of Followership," http://onlineethics.org/corp/leader.html#ethics.

Search for Timothy Within

I trust that you desire to be the best staff member, supportive minister, or volunteer worker you can be and are endeavoring to walk out the call of God on your life in a way that is both pleasing to the Lord and honorable to the people with whom you work. However, you may be thinking, *Okay, I've just read 34 chapters on what this "Timothy" is supposed to look like and act like and be like—now where do I start? How can I become a "Timothy"? Do I need to attend classes at my church before I can start to become a Timothy? Or do I need to just give up now—because I don't resemble Timothy at all!* I will give you the same foundational advice given to pastors in the previous chapter: Be encouraged…be patient.

It wouldn't be fair to tell you to search for Timothy and then not give you a platform from where to start your search. "Timothy" isn't some sort of garment you *put on* or something you find and then *possess*. Timothy is someone you *become*. Just as it took time for the disciples to be transformed by learning, doing, and becoming, so will your personal transformation take time. I can't tell you how long it will take to see the Timothy within you come to maturity and fruition, but I can give you some practical steps to take that will enable you to starting becoming more like Timothy everyday.

Practical Steps to Take
to Become Timothy

After reading through this book and determining what is present and what is lacking, you need to make a plan. We learned in a previous chapter that success comes when we plan our work then work our plan.

1. Make a list of the principles or traits you want to see active and functioning in your life. Go back through this book and highlight or mark the areas you believe need some work and attention.

2. Prioritize your list according to what you feel needs the most immediate attention. You may have a lot to work on, but you can't feasibly work on everything at once. Having a plan of action will help you to stay focused and patient throughout the growth process.

3. Spend some time in prayer, asking the Holy Spirit to reveal what your immediate focus should be and to give you a plan of action that suits your needs and disposition. While in prayer, ask the Lord for His wisdom (James 1:9) and commit your way to Him (Ps. 37:5). Rely on the grace of God at work in your life to bring the plan to pass.

4. Set some measurable, reachable goals. For example, don't write, "I want to get better at being punctual." The term "better" is difficult to measure, and you will be hard pressed to determine whether or not you are growing or succeeding. Perhaps write something like, "I will wake up 15 minutes earlier every day this week in order to leave my house 15 minutes earlier than I usually do. That way I will arrive on time and not be late." Not only have you set a measurable goal (did I wake up and leave 15 minutes earlier than normal?), but you also set a reachable goal in that you're goal is to wake up and leave earlier for *one week*. In other words, you didn't set yourself up for failure by saying, "I'll never

be late again." When setting goals for yourself, make sure they are *measurable* and *reachable*, and then go from there.

5. If you need help creating a list of priorities and/or setting goals for yourself, talk to a mature friend, your supervisor or pastor and ask them to help you. Let them know that you really want to be your best for God and that you want to be a productive supportive minister. Perhaps they can see target growth areas that you are unable to see. Furthermore, by asking for help from someone you trust, you establish a sense of accountability that will help you follow through with your plan.

6. Once you have a plan, begin working on one goal per week. Remember, Rome wasn't built in a day and you aren't going to become "Super Supportive

> ROME WASN'T BUILT IN A DAY AND YOU AREN'T GOING TO BECOME "SUPER SUPPORTIVE MINISTER" IN A SINGLE DAY EITHER.

Minister" in a single day either. Give yourself ample time—that way you have adequate time to devote to each area and you also don't wear yourself out to the point of wanting to give up on the whole process.

7. Have scheduled follow-up times with your accountability partner or supervisor, so that you are able to receive feedback and encouragement on how you are progressing. These meetings will give you something to look forward to and add the attitude boost you might need to keep going.

8. Don't try to do it all yourself. The disciples couldn't transform themselves and Timothy couldn't train himself. Allow your pastor's sermon messages to speak directly to your heart; listen for teaching that will help you in the areas you are striving to improve. Get all the training you can. Read God's Word, especially the

letters Paul wrote to his supportive ministers, with the intention of finding particular scriptures to inspire and instruct you. Most importantly, spend quality time with the Lord, allowing His Presence to transform you from the inside out. Rely on God's strength and grace, *"for it is God who works in you both to will and to do for His good pleasure"* (Phil. 2:13).

9. Get busy working for God!

As you put into practice the principles you have learned, you may feel the need to review portions of *In Search of Timothy* from time to time. It may be a good idea to read it through in its entirety once a year and to study how you answered the questions at the end of each chapter. Hopefully, your answers will be different from year to year and show marked signs of improvement. As you reread the book and answer the questions again, you will be able to see where you have grown and where growth is still needed. This will enable you to have a clear vision for yourself and ministry at all times.

Have a Timothy Attitude
Regardless of Your Position

Most people who serve in supportive ministry have full-time jobs outside the church. They are employed in some other field and simply volunteer their time at the church in order to do their part as supportive ministers to help the church body grow and function as God intended. Others in supportive ministry work in the church as their sole occupation.

Regardless of whether you are a volunteer or are compensated financially, I encourage you to always be a blessing at whatever level you can and in whatever way you can. Don't be concerned with the level of position, title, or status you ultimately fulfill. Whether you work directly for the pastor, for an assistant, or for a department head, you are still a supportive minister. And you are still a vital, irreplaceable part of the Body of Christ and of God's Kingdom plan. Not everyone will be the "top assistant," but you can still have a Timothy *attitude* whether or not you have a Timothy *position*.

Start Where You Are
With What You Have

There are three lies in particular that the devil tells to keep you from answering God's call to become a vessel fit for His use. He tells you that if something great is going to be done, it's going to be done a) by someone different than you; b) somewhere different than where you are; and c) with gifts different than what you have. In other words, he'll tell you that great things are *different, distant,* and *difficult*. However, the men and women who were effective throughout the Bible were ordinary people who used what they already had, tools that were easily accessible to them but powerful when consecrtated to God and for His glory.

- Moses had a rod.
- Rahab had a scarlet thread.
- Samson had the jawbone of a donkey.
- David had a sling.
- The widow woman had a pot of oil.
- The little boy had a few loaves and a few fishes.
- Dorcas had a needle and thread.

John Burrows said, "The lure of the distant and the difficult is deceptive. The great opportunity is where you are." Be yourself—use *your* skills, talents, and personality—and start right where you are with what you have.

I trust that you are a supportive minister who wants to become like Paul's Timothy. I encourage you to look within yourself for the traits Timothy possessed. For whichever particular traits aren't currently present in your life, ask God to help you give birth to them. For the traits that are present but need some work, strive to strengthen them. For the traits that are already thriving, seek to build upon them.

If you have read these thirty-five chapters and are now ready to quit because you feel overwhelmed and underqualified, don't quit. There is hope. Timothy wasn't trained in a day, and neither will you be. Remember, this book reflects the ideal to strive for—to continue to press toward. Be encouraged, and don't give up. You may think you aren't ready or called—that Timothy is some guy in Corinth or Ephesus or some far off place—but with God's help, a little courage, and a whole lot of effort, you can find Timothy *within*. And you can start today.

QUESTIONS FOR REFLECTION AND DISCUSSION

1. Do you currently have a mature friend or supervisor you can ask to be your accountability partner and to help you become more like Timothy? If not, who are some possible candidates and how will you go about asking them?
2. Have you doubted your worth to God's Kingdom because you feel that you don't measure up? Have you believed the lies the devil tells about great things being different, distant, and difficult?
3. List some things (talents, skills, belongings, and so forth) that you currently possess that could be useful in ministry when dedicated to the Lord.
4. Spend some time right now to begin working on the first step of "Practical Steps to Take to Become Like Timothy."

If you would like to contact the author, you may do so at:

Tony Cooke Ministries
P.O. Box 140187
Broken Arrow, OK 74014-0187.

You may also contact Tony through his Web site at
www.tonycooke.org.